LET MY PEOPLE GO!

(The true story of present day
persecution and slavery)

LET MY PEOPLE GO!

Cal R. Bombay

Multnomah Publishers *Sisters, Oregon*

LET MY PEOPLE GO!
published by Multnomah Publishers, Inc.

© 1998 by Cal R. Bombay
International Standard Book Number: 9781590528242

Cover photo by Natalie Fobes/Tony Stone Images;
Cover photo of Hand prints by Phillip & Karen Smith/Tony Stone Images

Design by Steve Gardner

Scripture quotations are from:
The Holy Bible, New King James Version (NKJV)
© 1984 by Thomas Nelson, Inc.

Multnomah is a trademark of Multnomah Publishers, Inc.,
and is registered in the U.S. Patent and Trademark Office.
The colophon is a trademark of Multnomah Publishers, Inc.

Printed in the United States of America

For information:
MULTNOMAH PUBLISHERS, INC.•POST OFFICE BOX 1720•SISTERS, OREGON 97759

148368442

This book is dedicated to the memory of those who have died in the faith in southern Sudan even when there was the choice to live without the faith.

──ACKNOWLEDGMENTS──

Without certain people, this book would never have been written. Baroness Caroline Cox of Queensbury nudged me into involvement. John Eibner, David Mainse, and Fred Vanstone encouraged me to go to Sudan. Those who made sacrifices in order to both free slaves and feed the starving in Sudan deserve the greater credit. I thank every one of them. I would also like to acknowledge and thank Nancy Schmickle, my editor, for her ability to elicit details from my memory by her probing and perceptive comments and questions. Last, but definitely not least, I want to thank my wife, Mary, for living through uncertain moments while I was in "no go" country.

contents

INTRODUCTION

The heat was like a blast furnace.

My traveling companions and I were in forbidden territory under threat of death, 450 miles deep in Sudan's dusty, dry interior. And I was not altogether sure I wanted to be here now that I had arrived. But I had heard the practice of slavery was still happening in almost unbelievable numbers in Sudan. I had also heard that slaves could be bought from their Muslim Arab owners in the north of Sudan and set free to be with their families again in their home villages.

Starvation had also become a major issue. The slave raiders continued to come—killing, destroying, robbing, and taking captives to be sold as slaves. To make matters worse, they burned and destroyed any food in the fields or in storage which they could not carry.

I had come to check it out, and as a Christian, to put it simply, interfere with such a horror in this day and age.

Now I was on the spot, the very one I had read and heard about. I had come loaded with cash for the redemption of slaves and, at the moment, this journey seemed like it would make better material for a nightmare. My weight and my age also made this whole thing seem foolish.

My attention returned to our upcoming meeting as suddenly someone spoke and everyone rose to their feet.

Several people pointed to our right. Coming out of the bush were two figures in immaculate white *jallabiyahs* (robes). They were followed by a line of women and children. Even at this distance, it was evident that the black people following the slave traders were poorly dressed—if at all.

My heart quickened. As I glanced again at the two white-robed figures coming toward us, I realized the line of women and children following them was longer than I had at first thought. Much longer!

Suddenly another voice was raised and arms pointed.

From another point in the bush, three more figures in white emerged followed by a long line of women and children. I heard Caroline Cox say, almost under her breath, "Praise the Lord." We had come to redeem one hundred slaves. This was beginning to look like many, many more than that.

Some were dressed in rags. A few had fairly decent and clean clothes. Most were barefoot. Although some had shoes, they were plastic and badly worn and torn. Others were nearly naked, and some were indeed naked, especially the youngest of the boys and girls. The women's ages appeared to be anywhere from the mid teens to forty. Boys and girls ages ranged from infants on their mothers' breasts to early teens. Without exception they had lifeless eyes. Some were nervous. Their glances at me and the other white people were uncertain, apprehensive.

They filed past me and were told to sit under the huge tree.

There must have been over 150 in this group alone. I glanced at the other line of slaves who were being seated under the second tree about seventy-five yards away and the gravity of the situation struck me with a paradoxical array of emotions.

chapter one

TAKING ACTION

My introduction to the allegations of slavery as a modern day practice was in late November 1996, when Lorna Dueck, one of the hosts of the Christian television program *100 Huntley Street,* showed me a *Baltimore Sun* feature on slavery in Sudan.

Louis Farrakhan of the "Nation of Islam" had challenged journalists to prove their allegations of the practice of slavery in Sudan after repeatedly being questioned about these allegations. During a press conference, Farrakhan finally challenged the journalists, telling them to "prove it!"

As a result, Gregory Cane, an African-American, and Gilbert Lewthwaite, a white American, went to Sudan with Baroness Caroline Cox and Mr. John Eibner, both veterans to the situation.

The *Baltimore Sun* reports told of the purchase of two young Dinka boys by the newspaper reporters. The boys were set free and gave an account of their experience as slaves. It was riveting material.

As the vice president of missions, I felt that we should address the issue Lorna Dueck brought up on that day's broadcast of *100*

Huntley Street. Some quick action was needed. David Mainse, principle host of the program and president of the Crossroads ministry, suggested we try to contact Lady Caroline Cox to have her input on the program by telephone. Just a few minutes before the program went live to air, we were able to establish telephone contact with Baroness Cox in England. David interviewed her and John Eibner in Switzerland that same day.

I was not quite prepared for some of the contents of the articles which Lorna read over the air. Having lived in Africa for seventeen years, I could quite ably, within the context of African life, interpret the horrors being reported. I have a deep love for Africa and its people and was profoundly moved as Lorna read excerpts from the *Baltimore Sun.* The conditions of slavery the journalists described and from which these two boys had been freed were horrifying.

The articles also mentioned that the price to redeem a slave ran about three hundred U.S. dollars. Somewhere in the middle of our conversation I made a statement, something like—"As Christians, we cannot know about a situation like this and do nothing." I cannot remember making any kind of specific appeal for funds, although the mention of the price of a slave may have triggered people's compassion.

The horror as well as the reality of the situation must have touched many people, and within three weeks we had received about $118,000 Canadian dollars designated specifically for the redemption of slaves. I had to make some decisions as administrator for the Emergency Response and Development Fund (ERDF). In my capacity as the vice president of missions and in consultation with our president, David Mainse, we decided to ask both

Lady Cox and John Eibner to come to Canada to talk about the situation in Sudan as guests on *100 Huntley Street.*

Baroness Caroline Cox is the president of Christian Solidarity International (England) and a Deputy Speaker of the House of Lords in London. By October 1997 she had gone to Sudan covertly seventeen times. She was once confronted by the regime in Khartoum and was told she could go anywhere she wanted in Sudan and was then flown *over* the areas she wanted to visit. When she said she wanted to land in the "no go" areas, she was told by the then minister of state that if she was seen flying into those areas she "would be shot out of the air."

John Eibner is the director of Christian Solidarity's international headquarters in Switzerland and works with the international president, Mr. Hans Stucklegruber. John makes the detailed arrangements for covert trips in Sudan and other countries. He is a very focused investigator and makes detailed documentation of the interviews, meetings, and agreements in connection with CSI as a human rights advocacy agency.

Lady Cox and John Eibner came to Canada and appeared on *100 Huntley Street* on February 19, 1997. It was not a lengthy segment of the program. David Mainse interviewed Lady Cox who, in a quite calm but clearly outraged way, told of what she had seen and experienced in Sudan, addressing the issue of slavery and describing the violations of human rights. A further appeal was made to Canadian Christians to be involved. I did my usual daily commentary.

After the program we had a private dinner with Lady Cox and John Eibner: David Mainse, our Chief-of-Staff Fred Vanstone, Mark Middleton of Emmanuel International, and I.

Quite frankly, I went into that dinner meeting fully intending to hand over our funds to Christian Solidarity International (CSI) for the designated purpose: the redemption of more slaves. We talked in some detail about the situation, including the fact that, up until that point, fifty-six slaves had been bought back from their Arab owners in the north of Sudan and returned by slave traders to a specific area in Bahr el Ghazal.

Our guests made it clear that these areas of southern Sudan where they were traveling were designated as "no go" areas by those in power in Khartoum, the capital of Sudan in the north. The United Nations, through Operation Lifeline Sudan and other humanitarian agencies, respected these restrictions on the basis that if they did intrude in those areas, the whole of the south of Sudan would become forbidden and no humanitarian relief would be allowed in anywhere.

During the course of our discussion I offered the $118,000 we had so far received, stating only that we would require an accounting of its use for audit purposes.

Lady Cox is every inch a lady, warm, quietly subdued in speech, yet forceful with a rather indomitable determination. She has a great sense of "mission" in her work. She looked across the table at me and said, "Cal, I believe you should come on our next trip to Sudan!" I was rather taken aback.

I tried to argue that my flight costs alone would purchase the freedom of five to seven slaves, yet secretly wondering, in spite of everything I had heard, to what degree slavery actually existed. Lady Cox insisted. John Eibner supported her. Then David Mainse suggested that it would be good to see it for myself and for a camera operator to bring back reports as well.

Under other circumstances, I would have jumped at the opportunity to go to Africa again. I had lived in Africa as a missionary for seventeen years with my wife, Mary; we had raised our two children there in their early years and I both knew it and loved it. And yet I was not naive about Africa. I had seen horrors and atrocities in both Kenya and Uganda. Even after leaving Africa, I had been involved in feeding the starving in Ethiopia during the great famine in the early eighties.

So, I felt prepared at least in mind, if not necessarily in body. Still...

Normally, I am not speechless. It was during what seemed like a long pause in the conversation that my heart spoke to me, simply saying, "Go." I felt it would please God if I went.

So we began making preparations. Obtaining medicines in case of malaria, cholera, dysentery, and a few other threats to health and life. Injections in advance, along with their reactions, and a pocketful of pills for various symptoms which might appear. John Eibner also sent a list of "stuff to bring." It included everything from tents right down to spare batteries and notebooks. And food.

I was also not in good shape physically, although I had deliberately lost over thirty pounds during the year before. I conscripted the help of a young neighbor, Eric Crew, into daily exercise in long-distance walking. Occasionally his younger sister, Jennifer, came along, adding to my realization of how "out of shape" I was. Eric kept pushing me toward longer walks every day. I'm glad he did!

One acquisition made by Lee Absolom, the video cameraman

going along, was two hats. Silly looking things. A bit similar to the sort of thing you see in movies about the French legionnaires. Back flaps, side flaps and a long peak in the front.

Before we left Lee became very ill because of some of the prophylactics which conflicted with medicines he took for migraine headaches. I found out later that, had he not discontinued one of the prescribed medicines, he would almost certainly have gone into a coma, since they were a dangerous mix with his migraine medicine. He did not mention this to me until we were well on the way. He was determined that he would go.

Phone calls, e-mail, faxes, plans made and refined, final packing of a great big backpack, as well as a day pack with sleeping roll and even a teensy little pillow. Everything was ready.

Within three weeks from the dinner with Lady Cox and John Eibner, we were boarding a British Airways flight to London.

BACKGROUND

To understand where this factual narrative is going, it is helpful to have at least a little insight into the past few decades of Sudan's history. I don't claim to have a complete grasp of all the background, either politically or economically, nor do I have a wide grasp of the ethnic diversity in Sudan. But I lived in Africa for seventeen years and that has helped me to comprehend the horrors of what is happening presently in Sudan.

In 1989, a radical fundamentalist Muslim regime led by Lieutenant General Omar Hassan Ahmed el Beshir seized control of the more moderate Muslim-dominated, but democratically-elected government of Sadiq el Mahdi. What makes the group radical is their determination to convert infidels to Islam by force or *jihad.* Jihad is a "holy war" that is waged either in defense of Islam or to spread Islam. Doctrinally, anyone who is not a Muslim is an infidel and a "legal" target for jihad. The moderate Muslims are less likely to make converts by force and do not want war and conflict. While the moderate Muslim holds the same doctrines—and theologically holds the theology of jihad—they are more likely to spread their religion through more peaceful means.

The southern areas of Sudan are rich in agricultural resources, gold, uranium, and oil. The regime in Khartoum wants total control of these areas to harness these resources to accomplish their own agenda which they have never hidden—the Islamization of the black south (turning everyone into a Muslim, in this case by force), followed by the Arabization of the black tribes (turning everyone into an Arab through teaching, marriage, language, and culture). If this were ever accomplished in south Sudan, the movement of radical fundamentalist Islam would continue its march south to other African countries.

This new rogue regime that is now in power is breaking every rule in the book when it comes to human rights and religious freedom. The black people in the south part of Sudan are dying like flies through deliberate action, and as often, inaction by the crazed leaders in Khartoum, Sudan's capital. Tens of thousands of people, the majority Christians, are now being used as slaves by Arabs in the north. In addition, approximately 300,000 people huddle in refugee camps outside Khartoum, having fled there from the south in search of safety. Over one and a half million have died.

By October of 1997, according to the information officer in West Awiel County, William Deng, 22,000 had already fled the camps in the north to return to their southern homelands. The reports of these ghettos of extreme poverty is beyond description.

Sudan was a part of the British Empire until 1956. During the rule of the British, slavery was illegal. In fact, all the laws of Britain pertained, but often in a strange but workable accommodation with traditional tribal laws. As with all laws, there are those who live outside of them.

However, slavery has probably been a part of all of northern Africa's history from time immemorial. Frowned upon by colonizers, but almost impossible to completely suppress, long-standing traditions like slavery die hard. Likewise, the Muslim practice of female circumcision has been practiced for centuries and is practiced even in North America by fundamentalist Muslims.

When the democratically-elected government was violently overthrown in 1989, the new regime took advantage of a popular wave of dissatisfaction among the people of Sudan and for the first while hid the fact that it was a radical fundamentalist Muslim regime by displaying a middle-of-the-road policy and thereby gaining the support of the moderate Muslims. Ahmed el Beshir, who led the revolution, had a collaborator in the coup, Hassan el Turabi. El Beshir imprisoned Turabi for a few months in a very comfortable setting for "show." When Turabi was released, he became head of the National Islamic Front (NIF), the religious and political power of the present regime. By then the junta was well established, having full control of the army.

It is helpful to understand that there are several "military" forces in Sudan. The Regular Government of Sudan army (GOS), the Popular Defense Force (PDF), which is recruited from moderate Muslim tribes into the *jihad,* and the National Islamic Front (NIF) which is the politico/religious arm with military force run by Turabi.

In the south, the largest resistance force is the Sudan People's Liberation Army (SPLA) led by Dr. John Garang. There have been splinter groups who have broken away from the SPLA through both tribal and personality clashes. Some of the splits have been over differences in the long-range agenda for the south of Sudan.

To add to the strife, there have been occasional clashes between some of these factions, and in fact, some have "gone over" to the regime in Khartoum being lured by political promises; few of which, if any, have materialized in concrete terms.

There have been reports that some atrocities have been committed by troops from the SPLA and other southern factions, and I believe it is true. In all the cases committed by members of the SPLA of which I am aware, John Garang has punished the perpetrators. When possible the injustices have been reversed. (Such the release of a Catholic priest taken prisoner who is now back in his mission carrying on his ministry in southern Sudan.)

Large areas of southern Sudan have been designated as prohibited or "no go" areas. Thus, humanitarian organizations such as the United Nations, Lifeline Sudan, the Red Cross, and other relief organizations are unwilling to go there lest they compromise their ability to bring humanitarian aid to other areas which are open for aid. From reports I have received, much of the aid in the open areas is manipulated by the Muslim distribution agencies to force the recipients to convert to Islam.

SURROUNDED BY DANGER

My thoughts were mixed as together with Lee Absolom, the video cameraman, I boarded the flight in Toronto and headed into the unknown. Lee carried two new Sony DV1000 cameras (new digital technology), and I had my faithful old 35mm camera. I remembered Lady Cox's account of her conversation with the minister of state in Khartoum: that she would be "shot out of the sky" if she was detected flying into the "no go" areas of Sudan. This thought kept nagging at my mind.

Lee was acting a bit strangely, which it not too unusual for Lee. But there seemed to be an added dimension to his strangeness. A kind of glassy-eyed lethargy combined with jerky movements. I commented that he probably needed sleep.

We had arranged to meet Lady Cox and John Eibner at the airport the evening of the day following our arrival in London. German army rations, arranged by John Eibner, were to be delivered to us at our hotel near Gatwick Airport. They finally arrived just a few hours before we were to leave for the departure hall. I had bought small cans of food and some quick energy snacks. Water filters would be brought by John Eibner.

We would be staying in an area where there was simply no

spare food and where clean water did not exist. John had advised us to travel as lightly as possible since all the extra space on the plane would be used for urgently needed medical supplies—and clean water.

We boarded a British Airways night flight to Nairobi from London. Our backpacks and bedrolls filled with all that we would need for over a week were checked in and we carried our cameras. We were scattered all over the 747 and slept fitfully through the night, except Lady Cox. She slept like a lamb.

We were met by officials of the Sudan Relief and Rehabilitation Association (SRRA) who moved us efficiently through immigration and customs. They seemed to have the right connections with the right people. Lady Cox, even in her jeans and backpack, was treated with some deference. When the few formalities were done we rushed from the Kenyatta International Airport to Wilson Airport.

Going through Nairobi was like a homecoming to me. The billowing black smoke from poorly tuned diesel buses. Familiar buildings, roads, and the taste of the dusty air. The flat plains reaching out toward the Ngong' hills. Egyptian kites flying between trees. I was fluent in the language that filled the air. The taxi driver took my Swahili for granted.

Wilson Airport is a much smaller but much busier airport that Kenyatta International. It is the base for TrackMark, a relief flight service that would take us to a small but growing staging area for relief agencies including the UN World Food Organization, UNICEF, and the Red Cross.

The place is called Lokichokio, and it is located on the main highway from Kenya to Juba, which is the major city in southern Sudan. I had been in that general area many years before when I had helped raise the funds for an integrated development project backed by the Canadian government.

Our pilot into Lokichokio was an Eritrean Christian. We flew in a Cessna Caravan loaded to capacity with medicines, bottled water, and another person who was a stranger to me. He turned out to be the Commissioner for West Awiel County in Bahr el Ghazal, Mr. Aleu Akechak. He was appointed as a civilian administrator by the Sudan People's Liberation Army (SPLA). I was impressed that the SPLA would set up a provisional administration for the civilian population, since the government in Khartoum had not only abandoned them, but according to reports were actually bombing towns in southern Sudan.

It was a three-and-a-half-hour flight north to Lokichokio. Our hope was to sneak into Sudan from Lokichokio and to land at a dirt airstrip near a place called Nyamlel, just before dusk on the same day. We would go in late so the aircraft could leave just before dark and get safely back to Kenya.

When we arrived at the airstrip in Lokichokio, I was surprised at the warehousing and apparently large population of Lokichokio. Just as we taxied onto the apron there seemed to be a great deal of commotion near a white DC 3. When we found out what was going on, it only added to our stress and sense of danger.

A NARROW ESCAPE

A group of people had just been rescued from southern Sudan, having landed ten minutes before our arrival. They were still on the apron and looked haggard and dirty. There were three white men and three Africans. They were led by Kevin Turner of Voice of the Martyrs. Still visibly shaken from their experience, they told us their story. It was horrifying, especially to our group, since we were to fly into the same area as a secondary destination.

Several days earlier, they had delivered food aid consisting of over 300 food packs to people being deliberately starved in the Nuba Mountains. We were told that the government army was guarding water holes to keep the people from getting water. People literally risked their lives to get water to stay alive. Some water holes were reportedly poisoned.

A GOS garrison, just fifteen minutes away by air, had somehow learned of their arrival and sent two helicopter gunships that suddenly descended on the unsuspecting crowd of civilians and the six relief workers. The gunships opened fire with 30mm cannon and shot about thirty rockets at the crowd. Kevin Turner saw, as he was diving for cover among the rocks, three women being tumbled across the ground by the cannon fire. One of the white men was an Australian who had served in the army in Australia. He described the precise weapons which were turned on them.

Amazingly, only four civilians were killed, though many more were wounded. The helicopters left quickly when a single civilian with an old rifle shot at them as they hovered just fifty feet above the ground strafing the people. He hit a gunman who was leaning out the door of the helicopter and shooting at them. Immediately the helicopters fled.

Meanwhile, everyone ran for cover, leaving everything behind. Huddled in the rocks, Kevin and his three coworkers filmed their final farewell message to their families in case they didn't make it out. When they finally returned to retrieve their possessions almost everything had simply disappeared. All they had left was the video camera, a Sat Phone, and the clothes on their backs.

During and right after the attack, Kevin was in contact with the 700 Club in the United States. He gave a live report over TV, which was broadcast across the country. With the same Sat Phone they contacted Lokichokio for a rescue flight. No planes were available. The only one not already in constant use was broken down. Others would simply not fly into the "no go" areas.

They, together with the African pastor and relief workers, ended up walking about ninety miles to another dirt airstrip, living off the land and drinking dirty, muddy water which posed great health risks. They could easily contract cholera, guinea worm, and dysentery. They brought back parts of one of the rockets to show the kind of shrapnel they had flying past them.

When we gave them cold Coca Colas from the cooler from our plane, it was the first cold and pure drink they had had for days.

I interviewed Kevin Turner on our camera. His voice broke as he spoke very emotionally of the thoughts he had while under fire, thinking that he would never live to see his kids again back in the United States. The other relief workers were from South Africa, Kenya, and Australia. They had lived through a terrifying experience. Naturally, their story did not put my mind at rest. We were about to fly into an area where their lives had deliberately just about been snuffed out even though their intention was purely humanitarian.

All this gave rise to ominous thoughts. What was I getting myself into? Would we get the same reception? Would we make it back out of Sudan?

We finally returned to the business at hand. The Cessna had been refueled, and we stocked up on bottled water and cold drinks. John Eibner was making final arrangements for our flight back out of Sudan, arranging both the time and place. We had planned on staying in Sudan for four nights. But then a problem developed.

The man who was going to exchange our American dollars into Sudanese pounds had not yet arrived. Apparently the money was not yet gathered and ready for us. To go into Sudan without the cash was pointless. We were hoping to free up to as many as one hundred slaves. As it was, we wouldn't be able to free even one. And we wanted to be prepared for more than a hundred just in case there were more who could be redeemed. Time was flying, evening was approaching, and to land on a dirt airstrip in Sudan at night—impossible!

We would have to stay in Lokichokio overnight. I don't know whether I was relieved or disappointed. We were each assigned a *tukul* (a grass-roofed house) in the TrackMark camp. We were warned to never walk anywhere without a flashlight and to be careful about scorpions. After a shower in tepid water and our last experience with a bar of soap, we had a fine dinner. It was a beautiful evening and a relaxing meal, with one exception—the occasional sharp crack of rifle fire in the distance.

We even slept in real beds. I heard more gunshots during the night and thought, "We're not even there yet, and bullets are flying!"

That night I opened my little New Testament, looking for some strength. For some strange reason, I longed for a proverb. I had all the psalms, but I wanted a proverb. As I leafed through the last pages of my little New Testament, I saw it. One lonely little proverb. It seems it was put there just for me. It was Proverbs 4:12 in the Hebrew version. It says, *"As thou goest, thy way shall be opened up, step by step, before thee."* From that moment, I had total peace of mind. Every fear subsided.

Morning brought us all to the dining hut where we had an exceptional breakfast for such a remote area. I asked about the gunshots the night before. The answer I got with a dismissive shrug was, "Oh, some differing factions having it out." This was from one of the pilots who seemed rather used to it.

John was finally in possession of the Sudanese pounds we needed to pay the redemption price. Someone had come very late the previous night, met with John, and exchanged the dollars. John now had a pile of about thirteen million Sudanese pounds. We could now pay for those whom we were hoping to set free.

By now, Lee looked like he should be in bed, but we drove to the airstrip anyway and in a short while Lokichokio was fading behind us. Within a few minutes we were in Sudanese airspace— illegally, according to the powers that rule with guns and terror from Khartoum. We flew past mountains, which contain gold and uranium, and over the fertile but marshy areas where the White Nile winds its serpentine way through the south of Sudan and then north into Egypt.

We flew over a government garrison a few miles to the starboard. I kept my eyes on the horizon, looking for other aircraft, remembering the threat of being "shot out of the air."

Several long hours later we were about five hundred miles into Sudan. We began a slow descent into a barren land where the Lol River was obviously dried up. There were some pools along its length where deeper water lay totally still and unmoving. We made a quick circuit, just about touching the tree tops, and landed in a cloud of dust on a dirt airstrip. The strip was about two or so kilometers from the little town of Nyamlel. We were now in forbidden territory. What would be our reception?

When the doors of the aircraft were opened, it was as though a blast furnace had suddenly been loosed in our faces. We were told it was 136 degrees Fahrenheit (52 degrees centigrade). It was easy to believe. We clambered out into the heat, staying under the wings of the plane as much as possible. The sun was merciless. I put on my silly hat.

Immediately we were surrounded by hundreds of people. SPLA soldiers armed with every weapon imaginable, everything from ancient rifles to modern kalashnikovs, stood around the periphery of the crowd. Grenades hung around the belts of some of the soldiers. Others had antitank rockets. They kept their eyes on the fields and bush around us, occasionally turning to one another with short comments, but seldom taking their eyes off the surrounding area. Some seemed to be looking into the sky. Some youngsters, also with guns, appeared no older than fourteen. Some were dressed in worn-out clothes and were toting old rifles almost as long as they themselves.

Yet there was a crowd of smiling faces to greet us, and there was obvious delight from the mixed crowd of people. It was a great contrast to the sober faces of the soldiers. The Baroness was the first to be hugged by many. The man from Switzerland was greeted, too, with happy smiles. The pilot also seemed well known.

Here I was facing a delighted crowd of thin, shabbily dressed Dinka people whose lives had been altered forever through raids by Muslim slave raiders. The thinness of the people confirmed what Lady Cox had told me in earlier conversations. The people were facing starvation.

The plane was quickly unloaded by these people who readily took the loads of medicine, supplies, and our backpacks on their heads and headed toward what was left of the town of Nyamlel.

We were introduced by Lady Cox to the local officials in charge of health, agriculture, statistics, and to the commissioner who led us on our walk into town. With cameras rolling, the Cessna took off into the skies. We would not see it again for *at least* three days.

We were all feeling the oppressive heat. Our mouths were drying out with every breath. It was March 14, 1997, and the middle of the dry season. We passed by the remains of houses raided and burned out in 1995. Rain had reduced most of the mud walls to brown and shapeless rubble. Any ashes had been washed away.

The faces of the people reflected the emotional devastation which took place when the raid by NIF solders and Muslim militia had destroyed the town. The raiders had come on horseback early on a March morning in 1995 and rampaged through the town, killing eighty-two people and taking 262 women and children to be shipped north on the slave train. When they reached the Arab north, the women and children were sold as slaves, or in some cases, given to Arab masters.

As we walked into the town, I was appalled at the total devastation. This place had been the British Administrative Center back in 1956 when independence was granted to Sudan. It had been a beautiful, well-developed town with markets and residences spread over a large area, perched on the cliff above the banks of the Lol River. Now it was rubble and ruin.

The town now consisted of a few rebuilt huts with mud walls and grass roofs. Others dwellings were merely woven grass mats supported by poles as a shelter from the sun. Little fences of the same matting surrounded small compounds which were obviously a family's "home." Few men were to be seen, there were mostly women and children. Both Lady Cox and John were recognized by many, and the smiles and handshaking told me that here were people who had developed a level of trust and friendship.

We were led to what at one time was the British Administrator's residence. It was one of the few buildings that still had a tin roof in place—or at least most of one. This was to be our overnight campsite. There was little of the original beauty of the building remaining, but the surroundings had obviously been a delight at one time. The building was perched at the top of a cliff looking down on the Lol River which was now one large unmoving pond being fished from dug-out canoes.

Lady Cox pitched her tent inside the round walls of a roofless, burnt-out tukul nearby. John Eibner pitched his tent out on open ground. Lee pitched his tent in one of the almost intact rooms of the old residence. I laid out my bedroll in a breezeway between the two remaining rooms, wishing there was actually a breeze.

We gathered together and opened our choice of meals from the German army rations. None of us knew what to expect since their contents were described in German. I ended up with a not-too-terrible Italian pasta meal.

Many people came around to visit us which made us feel more than welcome. One woman greeted Lady Cox by hugging her, and they both ended up silently weeping. I never did find out the story behind that particular hug, although I suspect she or her children had been redeemed in an earlier slave redemption operation. Strange thing about Lady Cox, even when she weeps, she retains that warm smile which seems to come from way down deep.

Someone brought us water from the pool in the Lol River, which we pumped through the filters John had brought. Darkness had settled, and all we had was our little flashlights. We said our good nights and headed toward our places for the night.

I had a sleeping bag, but I used it as a pillow, not wanting to get inside a sleeping bag in that overpowering heat.

During the first two hours I was in Sudan I consumed more water than I ever would have drunk in a full day in Canada. There was a well in the town, but it was broken down. I thought of the many taps in my house where I could get hot or cold water with the twist of the wrist. I looked at the small amount of water we brought with us, and a little bit of basic mathematics sent a shiver of apprehension through me.

SPLA soldiers were assigned to sleep around us as security. Some slept on blankets on the hard cement floors of the roofless porches. Others slept in some partially restored outbuildings with grass roofs. I was very thoughtful that night as I mulled over the things I had already heard from the civil leaders of the Dinka tribe in this little corner of West Awiel County.

This was Lady Cox's fifteenth illegal trip to Sudan. Her smile was permanent and genuine. She greeted friends with a hug and words of affection. Lady Cox remained a lady in any and every situation. Although now she was dressed in jeans and a bush jacket, she retained her calm and purposeful approach to everything she did, and she always had a string of pearls around her neck.

John Eibner had also been in Sudan as many times. He is a very quiet, focused man, almost never smiling. When he does smile it seems like an almost unwilling concession, yet it comes from deep inside. His mind seems totally focused on the task at hand—to get evidence of human rights violations, to write down every incident report, every statement by the officials appointed by the SPLA, to obtain statistics, and to record anyone who had a story to relate. He documented the needs of the people, the state of their health, the testimonials of their suffering at the hands of those who want to make Muslims out of the predominantly Christian and animist black population of the south.

I was told by Angelo, one of our main translators, that the people from Christian Solidarity International were the only ones who were consistently showing care and concern for these beleaguered people. More than merely talking about the violations of human rights in Sudan, they were *doing* something to show their care. We were told by the SPLA that they would defend us to the last man because of it. If it came to that, they said, when the last man had fallen only then would we be on our own....If only it did not seem like such a possibility existed!

I was notified by John Eibner right before this book went to press that Angelo's home village was raided while he was away doing relief work, and his wife and children were taken as slaves. Government forces were behind the raids, and they were specifically directed at civilians—Christians in particular. This was done simultaneously with the Khartoum government's announcement of peace initiatives and the opening of more areas for relief work through Operation Lifeline Sudan (a UN coordinated effort). Hundreds of people were left dead, scores of villages razed and livestock stolen. Lady Cox said it is the worst genocide she has ever seen.

Sleeping was a fitful experience. So hot! Thoughts racing. Dry mouth. Strange noises. What would tomorrow bring? Would my practice walking be enough to prepare me for the minimum of twenty-three kilometers we had to walk in this heat? How in the world did little Lady Cox do this over and over again? John looked wiry enough. Lee was sick. Throughout the night I sipped from my water bottle.

Voices quietly murmured in the darkness. Mice scurried about. There were noises from Lee's room—and then a crash against the door with some grunts and scuffling. I figured Lee was old enough to look after himself and left it at that. More voices in the darkness. Some near at hand, others at a distance, but subdued. I got up, went around to the makeshift washroom, decided it was too dirty, and walked off into the bush. I was being watched, but I knew they were friendly and protective eyes.

I thought a mouse had got into my food while I was off in the bush. I shone my flashlight on it and threw my roll of toilet paper at my backpack. Nothing. I suspected those watching eyes were probably now amused. I was. I eventually slept—I think.

In the morning I asked Lee what all the noise had been about during the night. He showed me. Mice had got into his backpack and had eaten away at a bag of dried fruit and nuts. He threw it all away with disgust as he realized what now might be mixed in with this fine Canadian snack. We had a quick breakfast from the German army rations which we had divided between us all. It was…okay…and whatever it was, I had never had it before for breakfast.

After packing our backpacks again, we went to meet more formally with Commissioner Aleu Akechak and his officers. I was told he was a lawyer who had practiced in Khartoum and had also been appointed as a judge there. When his people in the south began to be persecuted, raided, bombarded, displaced, and murdered, he decided to come to the south to do what he could for them. He was appointed by the SPLA as commissioner for West Awiel County. He struck me as a very thoughtful and caring man. Those around him took his instructions without question, but were also given the opportunity to express opinions and make recommendations.

We also met some well-educated, dignified gentlemen who worked with the commissioner: his deputy, Joseph Akok; Angelo Marach, coordinator for relief and supplies; William Deng, Statistics and Information Officer; Simon Kuot, nurse and local health coordinator. There were others introduced who sat as quiet observers to the discussions between Lady Cox, John Eibner, and Commissioner Aleu and his "cabinet."

John and Lady Cox wrote down facts, figures, and reports. It appeared that raids had lessened considerably since the peace initiatives taken by CSI between the Dinka and the moderate Muslims. Some of the reports were not as positive. Some recent raids had taken place not too far away. They recorded the number of people killed, cattle taken, women and children missing, taken as slaves. They had a clear picture of their whole area. Every person in the county was accounted for, present or missing—or dead. They knew every village which had been raided in the past, how many dead, and how many taken captive.

Time droned on, the heat was beginning to drain me. As they

talked of things and places I knew nothing about, my mind drifted. I was sitting leaning forward with my hands on my knees. A chicken walked between my feet into the middle of the grass-covered enclosure. No one seemed to notice. I thought of my big, healthy chickens back home in Canada and compared them to this scrawny little creature searching for anything to eat.

We were already a day late for the trek to the Manyiel area where we were to meet the slave traders. We were told that we might not be able redeem as many as the hundred we had hoped for, but the redemption of even less than that would be worthwhile—if they turned up at all…

As the day progressed, it was getting to be the full heat of the day, and the sun was a copper ball behind the heat haze above us. I found myself sipping from my thermos even as we sat still. Finally, we packed the last of our camping gear and most of it was loaded onto bicycles to go ahead of us for our overnight stay in Manyiel, the town closest to where we would make the "trade."

With my 35mm camera around my neck and one of the digital TV cameras and Lee Absolom with the other TV camera, we headed down the cliff to a path leading off into a plain of tall grass. Sharp-edged grass, mostly dried out. We could see wooden canoes with young boys casting nets in the large, unmoving pool in the bed of the Lol River. My thoughts were asking, "Can I make it?" The heat was oppressive. Lady Cox and John Eibner lit out at a determined clip, and I tried to keep up. They waited for us at a long shallow pool of what looked like clear water, although it had a few hidden enemies—crocodiles and diseases such as guinea worm, belharzia (which attacks vital organs and then the brain, fatal if left untreated), several kinds of amoeba which cause life-threatening dysentery.

Not wanting to walk for the next miles in wet shoes, we took off our shoes and socks and waded through the innocent looking water.

When we reached the other side, the sand was difficult to get out of our toes. It was essential that we get it all out. One abrasion could become septic very quickly. We dried our feet, put our shoes back on, and started walking again. The trail led through tall, head-high grass which grew in the flood plain along the Lol. The earth was black and like rock hard Manitoba gumbo. Before it had dried, cows had left imprints which dried as hard as pottery.

We eventually came to what appeared to be a river bank and climbed a few feet up onto flat, dusty country. The soil here was beige. Some bicycle tracks were visible in the dust and sand. Our backpacks and supplies, I assumed.

The countryside here in Bahr el Ghazal was not very different from other places I had seen in Kenya and Uganda. Thorn trees dotted the plains and there were low bushes, usually with thorns, which could cut deeply if you passed too close. Lush looking mango trees sprang up occasionally along any path, in spite of the heat and dryness. Other trees, with gnarled root systems, sparse leaves, and very little shade seemed to survive all kinds of weather.

Beautiful little yellow flowers could be seen on some bushes, incongruous in such an otherwise vast, dry wasteland. There were also pretty little multicolored flowers that looked like a cross between a snapdragon and an orchid, reddish orange with yellow petals.

We began to see people and an occasional mud hut with a thatched roof. Some goats, and even some cattle, were to be seen. Yet there seemed to be an all-too-common thinness to everyone.

Little farm plots near the houses with dried out cornstalks, the occasional chicken, and a broad-leafed plant, perhaps cassava, a root food. Small herds of goats skipped across the path in front of us. But the land was dry, dusty, oppressive. Hunger was a part of their lives now. I became very conscious of my own extra girth and how fortunate I was to live in Canada.

I had picked up a companion, about twelve years of age, in shorts and a raggy shirt. He said his name was Patrick, and he told me, "I now you friend." He insisted on carrying my small day-pack, which by that time I was quite willing to relinquish. He chattered on in broken English about our new friendship as he bounced energetically along on bare, dusty feet. His smile was glo-rious. His happiness seemed unaffected by the horrors he must have known firsthand.

Each large tree we passed seemed like a milestone, an accom-plishment, a victory. Continually sipping at the hot water in my thermos, I trudged on, not letting Patrick get too far ahead of me. He had a spare bottle of water, fresh from some springs in Kenya. Water seemed all important now, and I kept remembering the deli-cious feeling of my feet in the six inches of water we had waded across just an hour or so earlier. I began asking, "Have we reached half way yet?" The answers were ambiguous.

Lee was looking sickly and was lagging behind, sometimes even more than I. John and Lady Cox, who had by now insisted that we call her Caroline, had disappeared in front of us. We rested under the scarce shade of thorn trees that really didn't offer much respite from the sun. By this time, any excuse to rest would work for me. The bicycles passed us, going back in the opposite direc-tion to get the rest of our gear. We were told there were only twelve bicycles in the county, and that the one motor vehicle which had been in the county was commandeered for the use of the SPLA. We walked.

We tried to greet the few people we saw with the Dinka greeting, "Ebah?" and, usually unsmilingly, they answered in what at first to me was an unintelligible grunt, which in fact I began to use myself when they got the greeting in first. I can't say that I was smiling myself. It was hours of trudging through the hot dust and my thoughts were of water and of wondering how had I got involved in this after all and how much further was it?

REDEMPTION

F inally, Patrick, in the midst of his chattering, made a statement that caught my attention. I looked up in response and saw a few more people than usual. Another half mile and we came to an encampment of SPLA soldiers under some trees and in some derelict houses. Lady Cox and John Eibner were sitting under a tree with the SPLA commander Wool Geng, several of our entourage, and several senior civilians of the area.

I sat on one of the beds brought out from a house, grateful for the rest. Commander Wool Geng was in conversation with Lady Cox and John Eibner. One of the things I remember him saying was that he was surprised at how fast Christianity was growing in the area. He expressed gratitude for what CSI was doing when no one else would help them in their suffering. He described the suffering of the civilians who were dying of diseases which could easily have been cured had they had medicines.

I finally lay down on the bed with the ridiculous looking hat with side flaps and a peak over my face; sipping water and breathing hard.

Eventually Lee Absolom arrived, the fourth foreigner in our

group. He looked awful. I let him lie on the bed and began to listen more intently to Commander Wool Geng as small glasses of hot tea, heavily sugared, were distributed to all of us. It was surprisingly refreshing.

After I got my breath, I asked Commander Wool Geng what he needed most. He looked straight into my eyes and answered, "Prayer." It was not quite what I had expected. Under the circumstances I would have thought food, medicines, and even weapons would be high on his list. Prayer!

Commander Geng was very emphatic on several issues. He stated without equivocation that the aggression from the regime in Khartoum was specifically to eradicate Christians from the south of Sudan and/or to covert them to Islam. He said, "We will not become Muslims. That is the only reason I am wearing this gun," as he pointed to the revolver on his belt.

He went on to say, "We are actually protecting all of Africa against this violent fundamentalist form of Islam. We are the only buffer between the Muslim north and the rest of Africa south of us, such as Kenya and Uganda. The rest of Africa should realize this!"

I was a little dubious of such a claim at first, but before the trip was over, I couldn't help but give credit to his assessment. I am not really into politics, but this runs much more deeply than politics, racism, tribalism, or economics. This aggression was aimed at the heart of the Christian faith. My reasons for being here at all were basically compassion. Yet in the process I was quickly learning how complicated even this can be.

Commander Wool Geng told us that some people in this area had to walk hours a day just for water, carrying a four gallon plastic container on their heads back to their villages. He related that people were dying from the most simple diseases like measles and malaria. He told of infections caused by mere scratches which eventually turned into blood poisoning for lack of antibiotics and that ended up killing the person. So many pointless deaths among the innocent victims of a repressive regime in Khartoum.

Tuberculosis and leprosy were also taking their toll. He said, "We have good qualified medical personnel here, but they are unemployed because they have no medicines to use." We had brought medicines. He was happy to hear that.

I became disgusted with the restrictions of the tyrants in Khartoum who declared this place a "no go" area, using starvation, privation, and natural diseases as a weapon against an innocent civilian population because they were mostly Christian and animist. These people would not bow to the tyranny of Islamic jihad.

I was starting to become impatient, wondering when we would meet the slave traders. I was told they had not arrived yet. I began to wonder. Wonder if the slaves would actually turn up. Wonder what I was really doing here in this very uncomfortable situation. Wonder if this might be some elaborate fraud to make money.

Then my heart began to beat fast as someone came hurrying with the message that the slavers were approaching the pre-arranged meeting place. My first question was, "How far do we have to go?" I was bone tired and dry. Anxious, too, not now so much about my discomfort, but about how to handle what was supposed to happen next. Would it even happen?

Lee came alive at times and used the TV camera, capturing some of our conversation. He also took footage of some of the

SPLA soldiers and weapons around us. They seemed well
equipped. But what do I know about war? I've never had to take
up arms simply to defend my family, my home, my property. No
one had ever closed down the schools my children went to just
because they were Christian schools. My home church has never
been threatened by radical elements from another religion. It was
difficult to put myself in their place.

Some of these very soldiers became soldiers because their
wives and children had been kidnapped and taken north to be
sold as slaves. Their homes had been razed, their crops burned.
They had little left. We set off. The soldiers stayed put.

Although they told us it was just a short distance, it seemed
like miles—which perhaps it was. When we arrived at the two
large trees, there were just a few local people and a few men with
weapons, some in uniform. I was glad to see that they were SPLA.
I asked, "Where are the slavers and the slaves?"

The answer: "They are coming soon."

We sat and waited. Tired! Hot!

Three rough-hewn beds, with interlaced cowhide as "springs,"
were set at the edge of a large grass-free area under one tree. A few
poor excuses for chairs were brought. We sat and waited. Still
tired. Very hot. A little bit nervous.

Then someone spoke and as we rose to our feet, I saw a long
line of woman and children following two figures in immaculate
white robes; they had only their eyes showing through the starkly
white cloths wrapped around their heads. Then another line
approached from another direction. There appeared to be far more
slaves than we expected.

I was rather excited, and I tried to give a report with the camera turned on me and the microphone in my hand. I started out quite well, and then, as the enormity of what was happening around me hit home, I lost it with a throb in my voice and a lump in my throat and I gave up on the report.

As I was facing the video camera while Lee was recording my somewhat poorly expressed comments, I remember one man in particular. I noticed him when I looked over Lee's shoulder past the camera. He was looking at the incoming slaves. For just an instant, his face lit up, then as suddenly returned to a stoic blankness. It made a strange impression on me. An instant flash of a smile, but gone in less than another instant.

Two hours later, I knew the reason. He had recognized his wife and two children walking in the line toward us. Later, when I took his picture with his wife and family, that stoic look was still in place, although it had relaxed somewhat. It is very African. Don't betray any emotions in front of strangers.

I wondered what might have been going through his mind, "What have they done to my wife...?" "I wonder if they cut her?" The fact that she was alive at all was mute testimony to what had probably happened to her. Yet I'm sure there must have been joy in their home when they were finally alone together as a family again. Certainly, later that night I heard singing and laughter. The beating of drums. But now, before the rejoicing, there was a major exchange of money that needed to take place to buy back these people from slavery.

The two groups of slaves were gathered under the two massive trees, their great spreading branches each able to shelter three hundred people from the sun. The three slavers I was closest to shied away from the cameras. One held a blue cloth over his face showing only his eyes. His head was bare and looked very African, although when we saw his full face later I noticed he was lighter skinned with slightly Arabic features.

The other was much more apparently Arab and had only his eyes showing through the bright white cloths wrapped around his head. The slave traders were looking at us intently, shifting their gaze from face to face, African and whites together. Their eyes reflected fear bordering on terror. Lee captured the terror in those eyes with the video camera.

After all, they were in territory controlled by the SPLA, and it was the wives and children of these people surrounding them that they escorted to this place near Manyiel to "sell" once again.

Before sitting, we shook hands all round. We white foreigners sat in a tight little circle with our backs toward the great tree trunk about thirty feet behind us. The slave traders sat side by side in chairs facing us with their backs to the open bush. The first few moments were really tense. Everyone glanced nervously at everyone else…a moment I will never forget.

John Eibner began to speak, greeting the slave traders with Angelo interpreting into Arabic. There were certain formalities to go through. Social niceties to be observed. Mutual words of assurance. An attempt to create an atmosphere of trust.

We learned that one of the traders was under suspicion for collaborating with the Dinka and with CSI and had moved his family from their home for fear of their lives. They kept their faces covered most of the time and used aliases. They didn't want to be recognized, since one of their number had already been identified and killed by the Khartoum regime for buying slaves from their northern Arab owners. Turabi and Beshir's reputations were on the line with people bringing slaves back to the south to have their freedom paid for and their redemption assured. Freed slaves have stories to tell and the names and places of where other slaves were being held, used, and beaten.

So this was risky for the slave traders too, but the risk must have been worth it.

The next half hour was spent in affirming that the price was still the same—the equivalent of two or three cows. It had formerly been about six cows per slave or the equivalent in cash.

The slaves were counted again by some of the Dinka leaders who had come with us. Three hundred and nineteen women and children. Three hundred and nineteen people with scars, dejected faces, trying to cover their bareness with their arms. There seemed to be a submissive shame in everyone, from the oldest women down to the little toddlers.

The two slavers with whom we sat had been appointed to do the actual transaction. The other three slave traders waited patiently with their groups of women and children. I had brought enough money in Sudanese pounds to pay for only 220. There were 319.

John Eibner had brought money as well, and some were paid for by the local population. CSI arranged for the payment of the balance. The slavers had little choice but to trust us.

The first payment was made to the Arab whose face was covered except for his eyes showing through the gap in the white cloth around his head. Fifty thousand Sudanese pounds. I asked one of the Dinka officials what was going on. He explained to me that an outstanding debt had just been paid for a slave who had been returned but not paid for in a previous transaction with CSI.

He stuffed the bills into some inside pocket in his *jallabiyah*. It was important to maintain and reinforce the "trust" factor. They had to know they could trust us if they were to take this risk again. And, by the looks in their eyes, I had no doubt they were taking a risk. I also had no doubt that the profit they were making was worth the risk. But then, what is the commercial value of a living soul?

We then began to count out the money. Fifty thousand Sudanese pounds for each slave. Young or old, a life was a life, healthy or sick. As we counted out the money, I had feelings which were not becoming for a preacher of the gospel. I must admit, I had murderous feelings. These men were dealing in human life! It was repugnant to me. Yet at the same time my feelings were mixed with an indescribable elation at the thought of 319 women and children given the freedom to be reunited with their families and friends.... if their family and friends were still alive.

As I looked at the children, I don't know how often my own grandson, Joshua, came to mind. I looked at the mistreated little boys and girls under those trees and got a lump in my throat. I had a difficult time deciding where I should keep my eyes. I decided I'd better keep an eye on the money changing hands. People in Canada had entrusted me with thousands of dollars to do this very transaction.

The money was counted out in bundles from a briefcase and two plastic shopping bags. Each little packet of money disappeared into large pockets in the traders' long, white robes until they could hold no more. The plastic bags were handed over and stuffed. We handed over a total of thirteen million pounds to these slavers.

I became absorbed in watching the reactions of the two slavers as they carefully watched each packet of 50,000 Sudanese pounds being counted by John Eibner, then counted again by Angelo, then handed over to the slave trader who checked it once again. Each packet was wrapped in elastic bands and then bundled together in packets the size of a pound of butter.

In spite of their concentration on the money, the slaver's eyes shifted up and around at the people gathered around. No smiles. The transaction and counting was all done in Arabic through our translators, Angelo and Simon. When the money was finally tallied to the last Sudanese pound and stuffed into pockets and plastic bags, everyone stood except the slaves under the trees. They remained quiet, unmoving, and emotionless. There was the occasional whimper of a baby.

Short speeches were made by John Eibner and one of the traders. Each side in the transaction agreed that this was a good thing to do. The slavers said they would try to find more Arabs who would be willing to sell their slaves. No specific time was set for another exchange. Contact would be made....

I watched them walk off into the bush with the bags of money and their pockets full. They glanced back at us as they quickly started walking away. Their pace and nervous glancing down at the bags of money and their backward glances made me wonder if they thought they were safe. Thirteen million pounds was a lot of money, and by now, many people knew what they were carrying.

It was hard to define, or even contain, my own feelings. Fact one: These people were trading in human beings. My anger was strong, perhaps as strong as I had ever known. Fact two: These same people were actually risking their lives to return these women and children to their rightful places—at home with family and friends.

When asked why they were doing it, they had claimed they had been convinced that it was the "humanitarian" thing to do, and I partly believed them. But I was even more certain there was a fair margin of profit in the exercise as well. How much is anyone's guess.

They had described how they would approach the "owners" of these slaves, offering to buy them back but not necessarily telling them that they were returning them to the south.

As we found out later, some of the slaves themselves had been told they were being brought back to the south, but they were not sure they could believe it. Certainly, when they sat under the trees waiting for the negotiations to finish, they sat stoically, quietly, and with generally blank faces and without any expression in their eyes. From time to time, one would whisper to another, then watch us all warily.

These traders in human flesh had the guarantee of the SPLA of safe passage, knowing that this process could and probably would be repeated. The question came to my mind again, "What would I do if one of those in slavery was my little five-year-old grandson, Joshua?"

We turned out attention now to the slaves patiently waiting under the first tree. We stood facing this crowd of expressionless faces. Babies pressing their unmoving heads against their mothers' breasts, rolling their young eyes up at us with obvious apprehension. Angelo spoke in the Dinka language to assure their attention. Then he repeated it in Arabic. Apparently there were some who had been born in slavery to mothers who had been abused in this slavery horror for six or seven years. Their children had never been allowed to learn their own tribal tongue.

Caroline Cox, with Angelo interpreting, greeted the slaves under the tree. She was warm and smiling, gracious and loving in her remarks. She explained to them that people in Canada and in Switzerland had collected money to pay the price for them. She then introduced me to speak to them on behalf of Canadians who had paid for two hundred of them.

It should be kept in mind that the local villagers and families also had raised enough money to redeem some of this group of 319. They had redeemed others before this, and a trickle of returned slaves continues even now, as families and villages gather enough money to redeem another one of their own.

I'm sure many, if not most of them, had no idea where or perhaps even *what* Canada was. I found it a profoundly moving moment. I mentioned the love of God expressed through the Christians in Canada. I told them how that, even though the Canadians did not know any of them personally, they loved them and wanted them to be free.

At that point, I could not help but remember some of the letters people sent with their donations to free the slaves. Several families had written to tell how they had called a little family conference, parents and children together, to discuss the plight of the Sudanese slaves. This happened just before Christmas 1996, shortly after the plight of the Sudanese was first mentioned on *100 Huntley Street.*

Each of these families decided exactly the same thing. They would forfeit the giving of gifts that Christmas and send the money to me at *100 Huntley Street* to help free slaves. Other letters mentioned similar types of sacrifice; not with any regret, but with great joy.

Christian compassion is a wonderful thing. The Scripture in Galations 6:10 came to mind again: "Therefore, as we have opportunity, let us do good to all, especially to those who are of the household of faith." Not every slave we freed had a Christian background. Some were animists, and I was told that some were actually Muslims. We were "doing good to all." We have subsequently heard that there is a great turning to the Christian faith by many in the south of Sudan. Compassion, even without words, when done in the name of Jesus Christ, is a powerful form of evangelism.

Since I had not heard anyone say anything yet to the slaves that we had just redeemed them and that they were no longer slaves but free, I took it upon myself. I told them they were free; free to return to their own husbands, fathers, and mothers. I knew that some of their parents had either been killed in the slave raids or carried off as booty and were not yet redeemed. When their freedom finally registered, they broke out in spontaneous applause and smiles began to appear on faces, particularly on the faces of the preteen girls—perhaps because they were the most vulnerable while they were slaves. Some of them had been retrieved before they were to be circumcised.

We repeated the process under the second tree where the other three white-robed slavers had gathered their group of quietly somber slaves. They all looked like they badly needed a good meal. As with the first group, there were many whose hair had begun to turn a reddish brown, a sure sign of malnutrition.

All this took hours. I was becoming almost dizzy with the heat, and perhaps the emotions of the moment. But there was more to do.

We talked with the slave traders for a time, assuring them that we would repeat this process. We reminded them that the price would never go up and would perhaps be reduced. This served as a mild warning to them that they had better not mess with us, and exorbitant profiteering was not acceptable.

We bid them farewell, and they turned and walked off into the bush to join the other two slave traders with whom we had negotiated. They would meet and divide the money on the basis of their own expenses in buying and feeding the slaves (which would have been as little as possible) and according to their future plans for retrieving more slaves to bring south from Arab owners in the north.

There are some that have been critical of our efforts on behalf of these slaves, saying that we were just aiding and abetting the slave trade—actually encouraging it. I think it is obvious from the situation that our efforts in no way influence those who are perpetrating this horror. Their madness stems from a far different motivation. However, there is still the issue that we are paying for human beings. It was only later that I was able to resolve the tension I experienced initially as I became directly involved myself in the trafficking of human beings.

It helped me to consider Jesus and his purchase of our freedom through his sacrifice on the cross. I also thought of the story of the little boy on the beach throwing starfish back into the ocean to save their lives. When asked how he could make a difference with so many thousands of starfish drying up in the sun, he said, as he held one starfish, "It makes a big difference for this one," and he threw it into the life-giving ocean.

After hearing the stories of the slaves, setting them free from what they had experienced was not just theoretical, but personal. I didn't feel as if I were buying them so much as redeeming them. If some unethical person made a bit on the side then, so be it, but let *me*, if I can, make the difference between slavery and freedom.

One of the questions most often asked of me is, "What guarantee is there that the slaves will not be taken in another raid?" The answer is twofold. First, the devastation of the villages already raided leaves nothing much for the raiders to come back to steal: cattle, goats, and food are all gone. Second, the SPLA has gained control over most of the area where we freed the slaves, and raids are rare. They have decreased considerably since some peace agreements have been worked out between the Dinka leaders and their moderate Muslim neighbors. There are no more raids; this is in exchange for the right to graze cattle on Dinka land, which is more fertile that most of the dry areas of Sudan.

🔗

chapter four

TALKING WITH
THE SLAVES

We turned our attention to the slaves individually. Caroline Cox chose an interpreter, Angelo. John Eibner used Simon. Others who knew English, Dinka, and Arabic stood around each to correct any misinterpretation. No one seemed to mind being corrected. They all wanted to understand the experience of each of those interviewed.

They interviewed only a small number from among the 319. None of the slaves left their places under the trees. Although some seemed reluctant at first to tell their experiences, others seemed relieved to be able to talk about their experiences.

Meanwhile, Lee and I moved among them, taking TV footage and still shots. We stopped to listen to some of the interviews. Some were reluctant to talk at first, but as they shared their terrible experiences, they seemed progressively more willing to tell the whole story. Others answered questions reluctantly, looking at the ground or away with a shy, embarrassed look. I understood when I heard some of the stories. They had been mistreated and subjected to the most atrocious indignities and humiliations imaginable. In fact, much of what I heard was beyond imagination. It was loathsome and repulsive—totally beyond any human wickedness of which I had been aware.

Following are just a few of the experiences told to either John Eibner or Lady Cox as they recorded the interviews of the redeemed slaves. Lee and I heard many of these stories ourselves, but John and Caroline took copious notes on each slave's story.

The following reports contain the real names of the slaves, the real names of the Muslim owners, as well as the real names of the towns or villages where the owners live.

Ajak Malek: Ajak, with her three daughters, was captured in 1992 in a slave raid from her village called Abuth. When the Arabs raided the village, she tried to run away with her children but they were caught. Ajak tried to resist but she was struck with a knife. She continued resisting, but was finally subdued. She was finally tied on a horse together with her daughter Abuk. They were taken north and kept as slaves by their actual captor who had raided Abuth. His name is Omer Mahmoud and lives in Gumelya in southern Dafur.

The only food they had was the leftovers after the family had eaten. She was forced to become her master's concubine and was beaten with a stick if she refused to do what she was told. Her master's brother also forced himself upon her and fathered a baby boy. She said, "He just had fun with me. We want to try to get back to normal living and a healthy existence. But we'll never forget what has happened to us."

Akok Won Awuol: She said, "Two years ago my village was attacked. Many of the villagers ran away, but I was caught and taken as a slave. I had to work on a farm where there were about ten other slaves. I had to cook for them. My six-year-old son was taken with me. We were redeemed by someone from my husband's family who met an Arab trader and arranged my freedom."

Adout: Adout is from the village of Machar. She described how she had gone in the early morning for water for the morning cooking and washing. While she was returning she suddenly heard gunfire and saw villagers running. She tried to run, but was captured and taken as a slave to Adela, a village in southern Dafur near Daien. She was given to a man named Ibrahim. She was required to grind sorghum, but was only allowed to eat the husks. She collected firewood and carried water, and whenever she did not satisfy her owner's wishes, she was beaten. She has scars as a result of the beatings. She was used sexually, and an Arab fathered a baby by her. The baby was redeemed along with her.

Seven days before we redeemed Aduot, a man had come to her master and bought her. "They brought me here." she said. She also said there were six other Dinka slaves in the same place, including small boys and girls. She added, "Even when peace comes, we will still suffer, because we will never be able to forget the beatings and the horrible things that happened to us. I will try to forget, but I will never be able to be the same again."

Aduot added more. She said, "I am very happy to see you here. I did not know that people like you cared about our suffering. Seeing you showing compassion gives us some courage, and it will help to heal us."

Abuk Kawac: Abuk was captured from Unarul two years previously, along with her small baby who was still being breast-fed. The raiders tried to take her baby from her and told her that she had to help carry the booty. She refused to give up her child. Eventually she was given to another man named Al Ahadi in a place called Meyram. She had to look after goats and was only given scraps of food after the family had eaten. She shared the food with her small child. She said she was punished even when she did nothing to deserve it. She showed scars that had healed over the places where she had obviously been cruelly beaten. The master's eldest son often beat her with a large stick. She said she felt hopeless and thought she would never see her home again. She was forced to work night and day.

There was an almost eerie sameness to many of their stories, yet at the same time, they differed in personal details. Scars from beatings were not uncommon. They ate leftovers from their master's tables. They most often slept outside, sometimes in grass or plastic shelters they made themselves or sometimes with the animals: goats and cattle. Young girls did domestic work and if they were over ten or twelve, they would be used for sexual purposes. Many were circumcised by force, a female mutilation that is unthinkably cruel.

As I heard the various slaves relate their experiences, I looked over the large crowd and thought, "There are 319 of these horrible experiences." How can mankind become so depraved that he can treat other human beings in such sinfully violent ways? It was, and still is, beyond me to understand.

As Caroline and John interviewed some women and children individually, away from the main group of slaves (some of their stories were intensely personal and horrible), Lee and I were looking at faces, trying to imagine as best we could, the feelings that must be filling them.

Some of the women carried babies of much lighter colour, and when asked, they told us that the fathers were Arab and the result of rape. Some of the children had been in captivity for up to five and even seven years. Some of the children hardly knew how to respond to the questions and spoke very little Dinka. They understood and spoke Arabic. The interpreter walked with me as I asked questions of various women and children. Some were shy or ashamed to talk, especially to a man. I could understand that. Others answered, but often reluctantly. Some could respond only when spoken to in Arabic.

One three-and-a-half-year-old child was being cared for by several young girls. They looked far too young to have given birth to any child. I asked about it. They told me the child's mother had died of thirst on the long walk from the north. It was appalling to think about the 319 traumatic and chilling stories here under these two trees. We couldn't possibly hear them all.

chapter five

PEACEMAKING

B y this time I was exhausted—almost beyond endurance. My feet ached. The heat continued to be oppressive. I began to wonder where we were camping that night and where our equipment was. I was told it had been taken to the Catholic church in Manyiel, and was piled in a house nearby. I needed rest.

I never had felt "old" before. The walking and the emotion of the last ten hours had left me drained both physically and emotionally. I asked where and how I could get to where we would camp that night. I was near the last of my water.

I was given a bicycle which had been used to transport some of the camping equipment to Manyiel. Then I was pointed down a path. Lee decided to stay behind to record as much as he could on video. He had a lot of pluck continuing in his condition.

My tongue stuck to the roof of my mouth. I had only a little water left. John Eibner gave me some of his. He and Caroline stayed on to interview more freed slaves and to talk with local leaders.

I struggled up onto the most awkward bicycle I had ever been on. I was pointed down a path and so began pedaling in the direction where I was assured I would find the church.

I was greeted with smiles all along the way, which was rough
in places from cattle footprints hardened to pottery in the dryness
and sun. They said it was just a short distance. It was not. I had to
stop and rest several times; I also asked while pointing, "Manyiel?"
The answer was always a smile and a nod of "yes" as they pointed
in the direction I was riding.

At one point I was stopped by a Protestant pastor who, in broken English, thanked me for caring and coming. I was grateful for
the rest as we talked. He described the difficulties the pastors faced
working without resources of any kind, trying to help their people.
He asked for my address. I gave him my business card and he gave
me his address. However no letters have been exchanged since any
letter I might send would certainly be intercepted, opened, and
probably destroyed.

I finally rolled through Manyiel's marketplace and a while later
rode past all the unique and busy stalls where colorful clothes
hung out in the African sun. It was still as hot as ever. When I
finally rolled into the bare, sandy compound surrounding a
church, I was ready to drop.

Some teenage boys took me into the church and up onto the
pulpit area, which was simply the same mud floor but about eight
inches higher than the rest of the church. A Catholic catechist who
appeared to be about eighteen years old, William, came to speak
with me. A chair was brought for me to sit on inside the shade of
the church. I leaned back with my head against the mud wall of
this primitive, grass-roofed church. I had a new perspective on the
whole concept of sanctuary. William gave an instruction, and I was
left alone.

A while later, a large red plastic bowl was brought and set on the floor in front of me. Another young fellow brought a pail filled with water. It was poured into the bowl at my feet. It was murky. I was puzzled at first. Then the boy pulled my feet toward him. He tried to pull my shoes off. They were tied in a double knot so I bent over to untie them. He pulled off my shoes and then my socks. Then he put my feet in the big red bowl of water and rinsed my feet.... I was deeply moved. I don't know if I will ever be able to describe the feelings I experienced at that moment.

Then the boy left me alone, my feet in the water.

I have no idea how long I sat, exhausted, wondering when the others would arrive, wondering how Lee would fare, as sick as he was. He eventually turned up, white and wan. John and Caroline also showed up a while later—John, with his almost angry look and Caroline, still wearing and sharing the warmth of her smile with everyone she met.

Since it was the dry season, we set up our beds right there in the open compound. If their were mosquitoes, they were welcome to a few sips of my blood—I was past caring. Several roughly made beds made of two-inch sticks and poles and laced with interwoven cowhide strips were brought for Lee and I. John set up his tent at one end of the compound near the perimeter. Caroline set up her tent at the other. We all got together before sunset, opened our German army rations and ate them cold—if anything *can* be cold in 136 degree weather.

It was so hot that Lee and I found it hard to even eat. We were too tired. The Larium we had taken for malaria prevention was doing strange things to our minds. I finally stopped taking it.

While we were eating, we saw four little boys about four or five years old sitting nearby. When we asked about them, we were told that no one knew whose children they were. They seemed to respond only to Arabic. We asked what would happen to them.

We were introduced to the chief who wore a multicolored woolen *tuque,* a garment which would have withstood the most severe Canadian blizzard! The chief sat with us, and through another interpreter, told us he would take the boys as his responsibility until relatives could be found. We shared our biscuits and some packets of jam with them.

Before retiring for the night on top of our sleeping rolls, John, Caroline, Lee, and I filtered a few gallons of water brought at our request from the dirty pools remaining in the Lol River. Squirt by squirt we pumped the filtered water into our canteens and water bottles. Through it all, Caroline kept smiling, greeting and hugging people, and asking questions—forever asking questions and writing down the answers. Reports on this trip fill pages with testimonials and information gathered by John and Caroline. Documented facts. Recorded horrors.

When the time came to sleep, I was looking for my hat to help make a pillow. It had disappeared. Lee, in a moment of glee, said, "Good! Glad to see it gone—it looked ridiculous!"

I said right back at him, "*You're* the one who bought the silly thing for me!" Looking at the video later, I had to agree; the hat *was* ridiculous.

How do you sleep in a situation like that? The heat and the circumstances were too overwhelming. But so was our exhaustion. Lee and I lay down on the beds which had been placed head to head.

As we slept, we were once again surrounded by SPLA soldiers with rifles, handguns, grenades and antitank weapons. Just as I was going to sleep, I looked at the fading of daylight and saw along the horizon, a camel being led. I was momentarily jealous of the camel's ability to go long distances in heat without water....

We could hear the sounds of the villages around Manyiel. Some singing. Some laughter. It sounded like rejoicing, with drums beating, and voices raised. I lay on my back and stared up into the blackness of the sky. Every star was like a diamond glittering up there. Just before drifting off to sleep, Lee and I discussed the possibility of making a documentary to show the world what was happening in this forgotten part of the world. This kind of horror needed to be revealed to the world. This kind of thing should never be allowed to continue. The world needed a wake-up call.

I was jolted awake by the sudden beating of drums. I looked around for a moment, rather dazed. Finally I found its source. It was coming from inside the long, mud-walled, grass-roofed church. Voices suddenly joined the drums. It sounded like a few hundred voices raised in songs of praise to God. But this wasn't Sunday, it was Saturday! It was bright daylight, and people were milling around totally disregarding Lee and I, lying there in our underclothes. I quickly slipped shirt and pants on over my tee shirt and shorts and went into the church to join everyone there.

In typical African fashion, the men sat on one side, the women on the other, children near the front. Caroline, John, Lee, and I went in, ducking under the thatch which came to within three feet of the ground. We were ushered onto the slightly raised, dirt floor platform. I watched the children singing. Some of them knew the words; others simply looked confused. I asked Simon about that. He told me that most of the children who were not singing were those who had lost their Dinka roots and language. They knew neither the tunes nor the words.

They had been in captivity long enough to be Arabic. Now their real home was like a strange place. I realized then that these poor little black kids were going to have to face the trauma of answering to their Dinka names and relearning their language. But at least they were free.

After the singing of quite a few songs in which I recognized the name of Jesus quite often, we white visitors were asked to speak. Caroline and John spoke of our common Christian heritage and our love for the family of God world wide, including these in Manyiel. Then I was asked to say a few words. I gave them greetings from Christians in Canada, talked about how we are all redeemed by the sacrifice of Jesus Christ when we believe in Him. I then prayed for them, that God would bring their persecution and terror to an end and that peace would come to their country.

Breakfast was another package of the army rations which were becoming less and less appealing. But we *had* to eat. We had a long walk ahead of us to return to Nyamlel. I was rested but the heat was draining me and water seemed more important than food. But I forced food down and took delight only in the little packet of jam which was included with the exceptionally hard biscuits. There were some chocolate bars too, but they were more liquid than "bar." I don't usually have a chocolate bar for breakfast, but it seemed to fit the occasion. There were also little packets of orange powder flavoring and sugar. I added this to my canteen to take away the flat taste of the tepid water.

There always seemed to be another surprise. I expected that

we would simply pack up our bedrolls and backpacks and start the long trek back to Nyamlel. Remembering the distance from the day before, it was not an inspiring thought in that heat. Picking up our extra water bottles, we headed out of the church compound, strung out in a line.

To my surprise, we were led to another large tree under which chairs had been set in a semicircle. We were all asked to sit down. When I asked what this new development was, I was told we were going to meet with the local Arabs. "Arabs!" I said, "I thought the Arabs were the enemy of these people!" I received some ambiguous answer like, "Some are, and some are not—these are not."

While we waited for the Arabs to arrive, I was filled in on some details. The people we were expecting were all local traders. They were here in Manyiel simply to do trade with the local Dinka people. For myself, all I could think of was getting back to Nyamlel and onto the plane and out of there.

I was told the traders sold such things as salt, tea, clothes, bangles, beads, and batteries for torches (flashlights) and small radios. Just the day before, I had rolled right through the middle of the market and had not seen anyone whom I would have taken to be an Arab.

A trickle of Arabs, all in long white robes, moved in under the tree, sitting crossed-legged on the ground or simply sitting on their heels. Eventually about twenty-five Arabs turned up. I was a little confused. Many of them looked like black Africans, yet certainly different from the Dinka tribe. It was explained to me that these were members of moderate Muslim tribes who have been neighbors of the Dinka for many generations. A lot of intermarriages had taken place, but they were certainly Arabs in their own opinion. This was later illustrated by the way they spoke.

The local Dinka leaders spoke first about peace and the fact that they could work together and get along without fighting. "Peace is good for all of us" was a phrase often repeated. Simon sat beside me and gave me a running translation of the proceedings.

Then Caroline and John spoke of peace treaties which had been made between the Dinka people and some of the leaders of the moderate Muslims. They passed out copies of a letter in Arabic from Sadiq el Madhi who was the president of Sudan before the coup. It called for an end to hostilities. Caroline asked the Arab traders to read the letter and share it with other Arab traders wherever they went. Then John passed a picture around showing Dr. John Garang, the leader of the SPLA, sitting and smiling beside Sadiq el Madhi. This seemed to deeply impress the Arabs.

One of the Arab traders seemed by common consent to be the leader. He spoke of their desire for peace. Then others spoke about how they needed each other and how they had been deceived by the people in Khartoum. They said that jihad was not what they wanted. They simply wanted to be free to trade and do business with the Dinka people and to live in peace.

It became apparent to me that both Lady Cox and John Eibner had been deeply involved in this peace process for some time. They had brought together leaders of both Dinka and moderate Muslims, including Sadiq el Madhi, who had been cruelly tortured by the regime in Khartoum. I asked to hear more about Sadiq el Madhi.

He had apparently been imprisoned and cruelly tortured by the Beshir junta. He was made to sit on a steel chair in direct sunlight for hours on end. He was offered water to drink during these times and when he reached out to receive the water, it was poured on the ground in front of him. He was subjected to mock executions by being taken to a wall while a row of soldiers lined up with rifles. He was made to face the wall, someone did the "ready, aim, fire" routine—and nothing happened. He was tortured in other ways as well. But it seemed they were afraid to kill him because he was reputed to be in a direct lineage from Mohammed, the founder of Islam.

The meeting droned on. Names and quotations from other Muslim leaders were also used and recognized by the Arabs. They emphasized that everyone was a loser during periods of war. People die on both sides. People are displaced on both sides.

As this meeting continued I realized its importance, but I admit, I am no hero. My mind began to dwell on the challenge of the long return to Nyamlel and how drained I already felt. I thought about the fact that, if all went well, we'd have one more night of camping in Nyamlel, then hopefully the beautiful little Cessna Caravan would appear in the sky, land, and take us back to Kenya, to what now had in my mind become beautiful—Lokichokio, a bright spot in the desert. A place where I could get a really cold Coca Cola!

Finally the meeting broke up with pictures being taken of the whole gang of us: the Arabs, two Dinkas, Caroline, and me. Getting along. Smiles and handshakes all around.

Some of our local Dinka traveling companions had come to the conclusion that Lee and I were about dead on our feet. We were given bicycles to ride back to Nyamlel. Several bicycles had already been loaded with our gear and were on their way back to Nyamlel. I put my day pack, water bottle, and a ration of food on the rack of my bike; and with Lee, sick as he was, behind me, we headed out. We were following two strong Dinka men, both of them armed and on bicycles. We set out for the place we would again cross the dried up River Lol, then climb the cliff to the ruined building we were now calling the "Nyamlel Hilton." This return trip was much more easily imagined than done! I thought, *Now that we have bikes, this'll be a snap. The land is basically level.* How wrong you can be!

Imagine if you will, pedaling a bicycle with the rubber missing from the pedals. Add to this that the pedals themselves were bent at strange angles. Then imagine pedaling along at a good clip on a good solid pathway, only to be suddenly submerged in sand. Pedaling was useless. We had to walk, laboriously pushing bicycles through soft sand.

Now, add to that the fact that our tires began to deflate. And remember the dry mouth from panting and the thirst that makes you want to drink every drop of water you have.

Our African companions and guides pumped up the tires, and we set off again. We went down winding, narrow paths and were slapped on both sides by sharp-edged bicycle-high grass. Then we rounded a bend in a path and hit a patch of lumpy sun-dried hoof prints made by cattle. This rough spot wrenched the handlebars right out of our hands. This was not my idea of a ride home. How I longed for my old air-conditioned Pontiac, even if it did have 315,000 kilometers on it!

At one point I was in the lead with Lee close behind me. As I rounded a bend in the path, I took a bad fall as I hit some really rough ground. I went down with a crash. Lee had no chance to stop, and he rolled right up on top of my bike, then fell on top of me. We were so exhausted, we just lay there for a while. Then the comedy of the situation hit us, and we laughed almost hysterically.

We dragged ourselves to our feet, picked up the bikes and realized one of them was now bent beyond riding. We pushed and carried them to the nearest tree—sat down at the trunk of the tree and sipped water. Our guides finally came back to find us, and together we "bent" the bicycle back enough to ride—just barely. One of our guides traded bikes with us, and we took off again. We stopped more and more often—sipping water and resting. As tepid as the water was, it was enough to unglue our tongues from the roofs of our mouths.

Lee was beginning to look positively awful. White is normal for a white man, but Lee was *really* white! I have no idea what I looked like, other than totally exhausted. I felt grimy from the dust and could even feel it between my teeth.

Eventually we reached the incline down onto the flood plain, which of course was as dry as a bone. The grass was taller, the paths more winding, and there were more rough patches from sun-hardened hoof prints. There were a few sandy patches. I began to wonder what death felt like.

When we reached that shallow pool in the mostly dried-up bed of the Lol River, I positively reveled in the feel of water on my feet. But when I got to the other side, I had to turn my bicycle over to someone else who had come to meet us from Nyamlel. There was no way I could pedal any longer. We could see Nyamlel which was in sight at the top of the cliff about two kilometers ahead. I walked, or rather, dragged my feet to the base of the cliff.

There was a quite good path up to the top, and it couldn't have been more than fifty to sixty feet high. Yet I had to stop and rest three times just going up that cliff.

Upon returning to Nyamlel, I was introduced to a man, who in my opinion, is a real hero. His name is Apin Apin Akot.

❂

HEROES

I n February of 1995 Apin Apin Akot's village of Sokobat was attacked, sacked, and burned. Apin Apin Akot was out in the fields with his youngest daughter. When he returned from the fields, he found that during the raid many were killed and his wife and two daughters were taken as captives along with others. His daughters were young, one aged five, and the oldest daughter Akec Apin was nine or ten. You can imagine the sense of horror on contemplating what his wife and children were facing.

Mr. Akot sold everything he had left, the cattle and goats he had been shepherding and everything else he had. With a wad of Sudanese pounds he began a seven-day walk north, through territory dangerous to him as a black man and as a Christian. He was able to locate an Arab whom he paid to tell him where his wife and two daughters had been sold as slaves. He was determined to buy them back.

When he arrived at the home of the "owner" of his family, he was greeted with hostility. He said he wanted to buy his wife and daughters back. The Arab refused on the grounds that Apin Apin Akot could not afford them. Mr. Akot said he could and showed the money he had. After a great deal of bargaining, he was able to pay only for his wife and the youngest of the two daughters.

He had to leave his ten-year-old behind. He was told that she was worth three times more because she was intended to be a concubine to a family member, and that she would be circumcised soon. He was told to stay away and never return.

When Mr. Akot left, and his ten-year-old watched him walk away, Akec Apin said to her father, "The worst thing for me would be to die. As long as I stay alive, I know you will come back for me." She later told us that when she watched her father walk away, "It was a bad time. I couldn't even eat any food for days."

His five-year-old daughter had been tied on the back of a horse so tightly and for so long that one foot is permanently twisted and crippled.

When Apin Apin Akot returned to the south with his daughter, he was totally impoverished. John Eibner and Caroline Cox gave him the somewhat larger than normal price to redeem his daughter Akec Apin.

Once more he headed back on the seven-day walk to Darafat in Kordofan, facing every danger again. When he arrived in the north, once again he faced Nueri Omer, the owner of his daughter.

An argument followed. Nueri Omer said, "I told you never to come back, and you have come back!" Nueri Omer tried to send Mr. Akot away. "You were wrong to come back! We refused to give you your daughter, and yet you still come back!"

Apin Apin Akot answered, "You took my daughter at gunpoint. If you had just a spear like me, you wouldn't have succeeded in taking her. I love my daughter and you took her from me. You agreed to give her back to me for money!"

Apin Apin Akot said that Nueri Omer made him swear on the

Koran that he would never again come back, but agreed to receive the money in exchange for Akec Apin.

Akec Apin told us, "When I was captured my hands were tied with strong rope. All the bad jobs were given to me—grinding grain in the house and carrying water from the well at night. I was just given leftovers from their plates for food. If I was slow bringing the water, my master beat me [we saw the scars to prove this statement]. All the family beat me."

She had been told that she was to be married to the master's son later that year. Though she was a Christian, she was forced to join in Muslim prayers and to wear Muslim women's headdress.

Apin Apin Akot told Lady Cox "You created me again, like God, giving me new life. When you gave me the money, and I bought my daughter back, I felt as if I had been born again!"

As I watched this family: father, wife, and three daughters together again, though in total poverty, their smiles were as close to visible ecstasy as I imagine I'll ever see.

There are unsung heroes around the world. Apin Apin Akot is one of them.

Before our scheduled flight out of Nyamlel, we packed our kits and had them ready to load on the plane when (and if) it arrived. It was Sunday. I was used to going to church on Sundays.

We took a walk through the ruined village of Nyamlel. Angelo pointed toward the edge of the village and said, "The village was digging a pit for a new latrine over there. When the raid took place and when the raiders were gone, the survivors made the pit into a common grave for the eighty-two who had been killed. They were mostly men." Then after a thoughtful silence he added, "They kill the men because they can't make them submit to slavery, and they would rebel..."

We arrived at a little mud hut. Very crude. It had a small compound surrounded by a woven grass fence. Though poverty was evident—everything was swept and clean. A small cooking fire was glowing in the center of the compound. We were introduced to an old grandmother and her blind daughter who was the mother of three.

When the village was raided, they had run but the blind mother stumbled over a table, and they were taken captive. The two women were later abandoned when it became evident that they would be useless as slaves, but not before the blind mother was sexually abused. One was too old, the other blind. They were simply left to fend for themselves and find their way back to Nyamlel.

Two of the blind woman's children were there when we visited. She sat with her arm around one little child with a beautiful smile on her face, and once again thanked Lady Cox, John Eibner, and CSI for buying her children's freedom. She said, "When I was abandoned and my children were gone, I didn't have any reason to live. I'm blind. My children were gone. My husband is dead. What could I do? But you gave me back my life by giving me back my children." Then a twitch of worry crossed her face as she told us her third child, a son, had been sent to relatives in another village because there wasn't enough food for all of them here in Nyamlel.

She said, "I would rather starve to death with my children than live without them!"

As I said, on Sunday I go to church. To my surprise we were able to attend that day. The church was over two miles away, and as we walked along the bank above the dried up Lol River toward

the mission station, we were told how that when the raiders came
to Nyamlel, they had set up a mortar on what we had dubbed the
"Nyamlel Hilton" and had shot mortars into the mission compound.

The priests were gone. A catechist was leading the meeting
when we arrived. I walked through the ruined compound of the
mission. Walls without roofs. Other buildings blown apart. The
church had a big gaping hole in the roof where a mortar had
exploded.

But when I stepped inside the church, sitting at the back, I
was almost reduced to tears by the sheer joy of the worshippers.
Several women were dressed in the most beautiful robelike dresses
in lively colors. Most were in rags. They sang with typical African
enthusiasm. We sat at the back and observed. None of us understood the Dinka language.

At this point we were still waiting for the sound of the aircraft
which was to take us out of Sudan and back to Kenya. Nothing.

We were asked to come to the pulpit and greet the people. We
each took our turn. We looked into the faces of those Catholic
Christians as they listened and clapped in response to our greetings. Their love for God and devotion to Jesus was clearly evident.
As I was speaking, someone came and waved somewhat frantically.
I finished what I had to say, then prayed for the congregation. The
frantically waving man then told us that the plane had landed and
had already been waiting for more than half an hour.

This was dangerous—an easy target from the air. We hurried
from the church and took a "shortcut" to the dirt airstrip where
the plane was already loaded with our gear. The "shortcut" turned
out to be not very short. My exhaustion was such that I walked

more slowly with every step. We were encouraged to hurry and Lady Cox and John Eibner took off at an energetic clip. They were used to this. I wasn't, and Lee was getting more sickly by the minute. A bicycle was offered, and Lee refused it, probably in deference to my age although he said he felt too sick to even keep his balance. He insisted that I use the bike, which itself was a trial. Lee lagged behind. I sent the bicycle back for Lee when I got to the plane...where a cold bottle of Coca Cola was thrust into my hands. This was a temptation I didn't even *think* of resisting.

We made hurried farewells to the commissioner, Angelo, Simon, and others and quickly got into the plane, took off, and headed south to Kenya. I sat up front in the copilot's seat. My eyes searched the horizon for any small speck that might turn into a MIG fighter. Nothing. Lee was draped over his seat, sleeping between bouts of vomiting into a leaky plastic bag. He did not look well at all. But there were doctors at Lokichokio, and that's where we were headed.

We had several hours of cool air in the plane. It was delicious, along with the fresh sandwiches from the cooler. As we approached Lokichokio in Kenya, I literally felt a physical relaxation move through my body. Touchdown!

We drove to the TrackMark camp in the open back of a pickup and were checked into our own private tukuls where I immediately grabbed a bar of soap and a towel and headed for the shower across the compound. What a feeling. No hot water, but it certainly wasn't cold either. I dressed in clean clothes, lay on the bed, and began to get a feeling that maybe I was still human after all. What a contrast there must be between hell and heaven.

But Lee was very sick. It was late Sunday evening and the sun had set. Lee needed a doctor. None was available. He had already begun a course of Noroxin to "stem the tide" but was throwing it all up again and feeling feeble. He went to bed in the tent next to mine. I went to have some supper. It was beautifully prepared. I drank four bottles of pop.

Pilots who flew for various relief agencies flying supplies into Juba and other "open" areas of southern Sudan shared some of their horror stories. A cargo of boxes of chalk for schools was flown into one area, and the pilot described a little boy with a bloated belly from malnutrition standing staring at the piles of boxes of chalk. They didn't even have blackboards.

Another told of having to fly in a massive amount of fish line and hooks to one village—a village that was many miles from the nearest water. The worst story was of a load of gravel flown into a village for rebuilding some cement storage buildings—the whole village was built on gravel—tons of it. Some of the pilots naturally wondered just who was making these decisions.

I was concerned about Lee. When I went to his tent, he was not there. Then I heard him "heaving" mightily in the nearby washroom. When he returned to his tent, I sat with him until he finally drifted into a fitful sleep. I went to bed and slept soundly until I heard Lee fumbling about the zipper to my tent and mumbling almost incoherently. I brought him in and he tried to rest on the extra bed in my tent. He groaned and writhed and was as white as a sheet. For two hours I prayed for and with him. He finally drifted off to sleep again. So did I eventually.

In the morning, Lee got medicine from a doctor, and we all packed, ready for the flight back to Nairobi. The flight was uneventful with the joyful exception of me being able to recognize towns and villages I had gone through by car twenty to thirty-five years before when I was a missionary in Kenya. Kenya seemed so green and lush compared to where we had been in Sudan.

chapter seven

UGANDA

This trip was not over. I had been approached by a Canadian relief organization asking for financial help for emergency feeding of children in northern Uganda. Apparently there were thousands of refugees from Sudan escaping to Uganda. To further complicate the problem in the town of Gulu, there were many thousands of local Acholi people who took refuge in the town. This was a little difficult to understand. I had been invited to tag this on to the end of my foray into Sudan.

The next day, we headed for Uganda with Mark Middleton of Emmanuel International to see the refugee problems in the towns of Gulu and Kitgum. When I lived in Mbale, Uganda, I had gone to Gulu to teach a series of Bible sessions. It had been a beautiful little town.

Gulu was normally a town of about 22,000 people. About 71,000 refugees had moved into the area, some from Sudan, others from the countryside around the town. We visited heavy concentrations of people in crowded mud shacks where the Church of Uganda was valiantly trying to provide teaching, food, and health services. They were holding a class of about thirty-five children on a decrepit porch of a house. Most of them were half or totally naked. Teachers were teaching the rudiments of the alphabet and singing. With the thousands of children roaming the streets in Gulu, any distraction which would keep the children occupied was more than welcome. That it was "school" was a happy experience for the parents.

We visited many places in Gulu. One of them was an emergency feeding program in the compound of the bishop's house which had been totally destroyed by the "Lord's Resistance Army." More about that later.

I decided right there on the spot to send $30,000 from our Emergency Response and Development Fund to help feed the children after I saw a group of over one thousand being fed their one meal of the day. It was cooked in big pots out in the open, and each child eagerly accepted a plastic plate with *ugali* and some vegetables.

Volunteers cooked and organized the children, giving special attention to those pointed out by a nurse as needing extra food because of malnutrition. Lactating mothers were given extra nutrition as well.

Many thousands of others were fending for themselves, camping on people's front doorsteps, scouring the countryside during the day for firewood to sell so they could buy some food for their families. It was heartbreaking.

While there in Gulu, I talked with the Right Reverend Macleard Maker Ochola, Bishop of the Diocese of Kitgum of the Church of Uganda. Although in very poor health himself, he was daily ministering to those in need from the little he had. His wife was fully involved with him in his ministry.

We were put up in "the" hotel in Gulu. The other "good" hotel in town had burned. The town was in terrible shape. I had been there on a teaching mission over thirty years before, and at that time it was a placid and lush place. Now it was ruts, dust, decaying buildings, and it was overcrowded beyond belief.

When Lee and I checked into the room, Lee took one sagging bed, I took the other. It was not a hotel a person would ever return to voluntarily—a rough cement floor, walls of cracked plaster, and cobwebs hanging from the partly fallen ceiling. A drunken party kept us awake until about 2 A.M., not to mention the little things scurrying around the room. Lee was still sick. I was now starting a course of Noroxin my doctor had given me in advance in Canada just in case—the "case" was now.

The next morning we visited the local hospital, St. Mary's Hospital—Lawr. There were only two doctors there. One, Dr. Matthew Lukwiya, had been kidnapped along with several nurses by Joseph Kony, a former Catholic choirboy turned rebel. He called his gang of rebels the "Lord's Resistance Army." What a misnomer! It's certainly not the Lord's. And they are not resisting anyone; they are attacking innocent Ugandan civilians.

Kony wants to bring the government of President Yoweri Museveni of Uganda to its knees. His "headquarters" are in southern Sudan. He is encouraged and supplied with arms by the Khartoum government. According to leaders in Gulu, this is a deliberate attempt to destabilize the north of Uganda, particularly the Acholi tribe.

Kony held Dr. Matthew Lukwiya and the nurses for ransom, wanting medicines for his ragtag army. After several days, when Dr. Lukwiya finally convinced Kony that he could not get more than a day's issue of medicines at a time since that was how it was supplied to the hospital, Kony released him and the nurses.

Dr. Lukwiya returned to his duties at the severely overcrowded hospital in Gulu. During the days of his captivity, the doctor had ample time to observe Kony. He is convinced that, as he put it, "Kony is a madman, with severe personality disorders."

Joseph Kony, himself an Acholi, has appointed himself as head of the "Lord's Resistance Army." He kidnaps young teens from his own Acholi tribe in Uganda and takes them into Sudan where he brainwashes them. Then he trains them in the use of arms and sends them back on raiding parties into Uganda against their own people. They terrorize the whole countryside, and as a result the people living there leave their homes, crops, and cattle, fleeing to the comparative safety of Gulu.

However, even here the hospital was pockmarked with bullets. Rose, one of the women's leaders of the church in the Diocese of Uganda, took her son out of the hospital because he was almost shot through the window by Kony's gang of teenaged terrorists. He died later at home.

Kony developed his own ten commandments, some of which are—you shall not kill black chickens, you shall not walk on Fridays, and you shall not raise white chickens. The other seven are just as ludicrous. Kony's intention is to take over Uganda and rule it according to his own ten commandments.

Kony's army is sometimes referred to as a Christian fundamentalist group. This is as ludicrous as his ten commandments. At the time of writing, Kony had abducted a minimum of three thousand children between the ages of twelve and fifteen. He turns the boys into killers, the girls become sexual slaves.

I met and talked with one fifteen-year-old boy in Gulu who

had been abducted by one of Kony's young terrorist gangs. He was then trained and sent back into Uganda to take part in a raid for more young children. This particular raiding party ran into the Ugandan army. The boy was shot in the arm and captured. He showed me the wound. I was told by the man who interpreted my conversation with him that the Army patched him up, questioned him, then released him into the custody of his mother. The poor child seemed totally bewildered by all that was happening to him.

We visited a former recreation center which was now refuge to a huge number of families camped out along the inside walls. There was not room enough for all, and others were out under the verandah's roof. St. Mary's Hospital–Lawr also opened its compound at night to accommodate many, who slept out in the open. It was a heart-wrenching sight to see families that evening struggling to stake out a small space where they could at least be together with the few shabby belongings they carried wherever they went.

We had Missionary Aviation Fellowship fly us to Gulu, and we now flew over to Kitgum. On our way we flew over several refugee camps that from the air looked very orderly, but when we landed and saw them close up, they looked like concentrated health hazards.

In Kitgum, at the top of a hill, we came to what was once a beautiful hotel. It was now crowded beyond capacity with refugees, and a large makeshift refugee camp with thousands of people was spread out across the top of the hill. Water was being pumped up the hill for drinking and washing, and food was being provided by the United Nations from a large efficiently run warehouse. But the people looked hopeless.

When I had talked with the Bishop of Kitgum, The Rt. Rev. Macleord Maker Ochola, while I was in Gulu, he had described the efforts the Church of Uganda was making to try to help the people. But it was woefully short of the needs. I have seldom seen a pastor more dedicated to the needs of his people than Rev. Ochola.

Only a few months later I received a letter from him telling me of the brutal death of his wife, Winifred, by a land mine planted by the rebels of Joseph Kony's "Lord's Resistance Army." It happened just outside of Kitgum.

Rev. Ochola wrote at the close of his letter, "May the good Lord graciously forgive all those who have bereaved me and the family in this unthinkable manner. May her soul rest in peace with all the saints who are already with the Lord in eternity."

When we were about to leave Kitgum on the M.A.F. plane, some relief workers attempted to commandeer our plane. They said it was urgent. They gave no reason for the urgency, but we finally found out they were afraid, quite understandably, to go by road to their destination because of the land mines they knew were along the roads. We had leased the plane, and we had to get to Entebbe, which is in the south of Uganda on the shores of Lake Nyanza (formerly Lake Victoria).

While in Entebbe, we stayed in a clean, modern hotel and slept on clean, smooth sheets. I had the best meal I had had in a week—a hamburger with chips. We met and had fellowship with missionaries we knew who drove to the hotel to see us, the Garry Skinners. It felt almost strange to see such normal life once again after what had happened over the past week.

Our return to Canada was via Nairobi and London, England. Lee stayed on in England with an uncle for a few days, recuperating. I went on to Toronto. Even an aircraft seat in economy felt delicious. I had no idea what I would face when I got home.

THE MEDIA

I was exhausted when I returned to Canada. We decided, because of the enormity of the violations of human rights and because of the number of slaves we were able to redeem, that we should have a press conference. We would release about seven minutes of video footage to the television networks. It was, if memory serves me well, Tuesday, April 1, when we held the press conference.

I must admit, I was nervous. I had never been a part of a press conference in my life. Reporters came with their TV cameras. Others represented newspapers or radio stations. The reporters sat on chairs in a group in our "studio A." The short video clip was shown, and then I read a brief statement I had prepared in advance.

After that, I opened it for questions. With one exception, the questions were straightforward and to the point. Only one reporter tried to put words in my mouth, trying to force me into stating that the whole affair was simply and only a Christian versus Muslim matter. I stated that my approach to the matter was certainly Christian, but not an anti-Muslim position. He kept at me. He seemed determined not to accept that what I was involved in was simply compassionate and humanitarian.

A reporter and cameraman turned up at my home that night, took pictures, and interviewed me. I was shocked to see my picture on the front page of the *Hamilton Spectator* the next day. People from across Canada sent articles they clipped from their local newspapers. A few days later someone who had been in Paris, France, told David Mainse, president of Crossroads Christian Communications Inc., that he had seen our footage on French TV.

In the next few days I did more interviews for television, radio, and newspapers than I can remember. John McCann from the Crossroads staff was my guide and mentor through this new experience.

During the radio interview with Michael Corin on CFRB in Toronto, after the subject was introduced, the phones were opened for questions or comments. One particular call was very significant to me. The caller identified himself as a Muslim and stated that his religion called for the killing of infidels (anyone who was not a Muslim). It was said in such a matter-of-fact way, that I was stunned. I was in Canada on Canadian radio and was told that killing was not only acceptable, but formed a part of the teaching of Islam. I felt that the majority of Muslims in Canada might disagree with him.

Another interview at 8:00 P.M. with Alison Smith on a CBC program called *The Lead,* lasted ten minutes. I told my story. Then by microwave relay, they had the attaché of the Sudan Embassy in Ottawa try to rebut my story. I was not expecting this and had not been warned that it would happen. I watched it from another room in the CBC studio. Alison Smith was very gracious, but pointed in her questions to the attaché. His answers were almost childish. He first denied I was in Sudan and then stated that "those pictures [shown on TV] could have been taken in Canada." Then he went on to say that I was in Sudan illegally. I had never denied that. Then he went on in trivial ways to defend his country, which of course he is paid to do; that is, not to be trivial, but to defend his country.

Then to my further surprise, Gregory Cane, the Afro-American whose articles had got me involved in this, was brought on for the last ten minutes. Gregory left no doubt in anyone's mind that he backed what I said as 100 percent true. He left the attaché's arguments and claims in shreds.

I am quite used to sitting in front of a television camera every day and doing what is called "Cal's Commentary" for the *100 Huntley Street* program. But I was not used to all the media attention I got over this, nor was I looking for it.

When I got back to my office one day after a number of interviews, my voice mail was filled with messages from reporters wanting interviews, most of which I found time to do.

I did interviews by telephone for Europe, the United States, and Canada for both newspapers and radio. One thing I was glad about was that somebody was paying some attention to what is happening in Sudan. These horrors must be brought to the attention of the world and brought to an end!

One of the messages on my voice mail was from a caller who identified himself as Muhammad Musa. His accent was that of someone who had just learned English. He said he was a Muslim, and that he had been watching the news both on TV and in the newspapers and commended me for revealing what was happening in Sudan. He ended up by repeating over and over again, as he began to cry, "Thank you...thank you...thank you." With a sob, he hung up his phone. I have kept an audio copy of that cry; he was a Muslim refugee from Sudan.

Literally hundreds of people contacted me, most of them thanking me for the information, although some of them called with thinly-veiled threats and accusations. Others claimed I was simply manufacturing outright lies. Some even said I was trying to defame Louis Farrakhan about whom I knew close to nothing at that time.

Then I began to get some really nasty reactions.

The Sudanese Embassy in Ottawa issued a press release denying everything I said, referring sarcastically to me as St. Bombay. It was written in very poor English and suggested that I was the *cause* of the slave trade; it made childishly sarcastic remarks about my activities in Sudan; and went on further, stating, "Would it not have been more religious, moral, useful, and humane to have a hospital and orphanage or a church built there with the good Canadians' assets?"

The fact that the NIF had burned down churches, bombed civilians, and shut down the schools in southern Sudan was never mentioned—of course.

They also never mentioned the reports by the United Nations Special Rapporteur, Mr. Gasper Biro. Mr. Biro reports in detail on the very things the Sudanese Embassy was denying. In Mr. Biro's report of February 3, 1997, he lists seventeen specific areas of violations of human rights by the Sudanese government. The first item on the list is slavery. This is followed by bombardments, amputations, arrests, torture and lack of due process of law, hostage-taking, reports of summary executions, freedom of religion and conscience, just to mention a few.

The report is twenty-one pages in length, was printed for general distribution, and was a result of a resolution of the UN Commission on Human Rights.

After I read the press release to my wife, Mary, she came up with a classic notion. "If they think it would have been good to spend the 'good Canadians' assets" on a hospital, why don't you offer to do it?" So I did!

I wrote to the Sudan Embassy, and I thanked them for their suggestions and asked what would be the proper protocol to get permission to build a clinic in southern Sudan. I said I would be happy to take them up on their suggestion. I never received a reply.

Wanting to keep the issue before the public, we asked Baroness Caroline Cox to come by way of Canada on her way to speak to the U.S. Commission on Human Rights. We asked her to stop in Canada overnight and we arranged for several interviews. We were short of time, but Caroline did a few interviews including one with Michael Corin on CFRB in Toronto. A major newspaper chain also interviewed her. We then headed for Ottawa with John McCann as our escort and guide.

We met with Paul Steckle, MP for Huron-Bruce who helped us to arrange to have a standing order introduced in Parliament regarding the violent abuses of human rights in Sudan. A standing order is an official document acknowledging the facts as presented. This becomes a part of the written history of the Canadian Parliament. I remember the concentration; three of us huddled over the computer as Paul's executive assistant, Terry Puerstl, keyed in the wording for the standing order. Several quick revisions and amendments, and we had it ready.

Then we were taken to meet the Speaker of the House, the Honorable Gilbert Parent, who invited us all into his private chambers next to his office. A camera crew came in to record some of the conversation.

After that we were taken to the member's dining room where we sat at lunch with a number of prominent MPs. In the afternoon we were taken into the House of Parliament and sat in the Speaker's balcony guest section. The Prime Minister, Jean Chretien, sat exactly opposite us as leader of the government. Baroness Cox was introduced to the House as a Deputy Speaker of the House of Lords of London and received a standing ovation. She smiled that warm and winning smile as she stood up in the balcony.

We then had a scheduled meeting with Christine Stewart, then the Secretary of State for Africa. Lady Cox presented her request that Canada take some action to condemn the Sudan for its violations of human rights. She spoke very lucidly and with quiet confidence. We brought up the matter of Canadian companies doing business in Sudan—businesses that could bring huge profits to the regime that was killing it's own citizens on the fanatical basis of radical fundamentalist Islamic jihad—and the lust for money at the cost of southern lives.

The only answer we got was, "Our hands are tied."

Nonsense!

Did we accomplish anything? Perhaps. At least a standing order was introduced to Parliament and became a part of the Hansard. I still am waiting for Canada, whose reputation and record on human rights is normally outstanding throughout the world, to do something. To even *say* something!

Although the United States has imposed only one sanction

against Sudan—the U.S. export of computers, an almost meaningless embargo for a country whose own primary export to the U.S. is gum arabic—there is some congressional movement to establish criteria to punish and monitor human rights abuses. As a result of testimony about human rights violations in Sudan, China, Tibet, and other areas, bills are under consideration in Congress which would establish an office for monitoring religious persecution world wide.

The United States House of Representatives passed a bill in May 1998, the Freedom from Religious Persecution Act, which would impose sanctions on foreign governments engaged in religious persecution. This bill would establish a new set of criteria under which the State Department must monitor and punish human rights abusers. The U.S. Senate will consider several versions of the bill later this year. Although there is interest in this area and strong congressional support at least in the House of Representatives in defiance of both the business community and the Clinton administration, progress is slow and uncertain. News reports suggest that White House officials have recommended the president veto the measure in its current form.

I had said to myself while in Sudan, because of the very great heat and exhaustion, that I would not go back. I'd let someone younger do it. After all, I was closing in on sixty and being somewhat overweight...

But during the many speaking engagements which followed, I was vividly reminding myself of the needs of the people of southern Sudan. For freedom. For food. People were starving to death by the thousands. I mentioned the need for food on *100 Huntley Street* and money began to come in designated for food and medicines.

I contacted John Eibner in Switzerland, and that began a new phase in my involvement in the human sufferings of hundreds of thousands of people. People needed food. Both John and Lady Cox had confirmed that there was mass starvation in several parts of Sudan, especially in the Nuba Mountains.

The threat of death once more motivated me to look into what I could do to feed those starving people in the areas where the rogue regime in Khartoum has heartlessly forbidden foreign aid workers to go in with humanitarian aid.

As our trip started, we were not reassured when we met Kevin Turner of Voice of the Martyrs and five others. The Government of Sudan army shelled them with 30mm cannons and rockets as they were delivering food aid to the starving in the Nuba Mountains. They had just been retrieved from Sudan, having walked over ninety miles, living off the land and drinking what water they could find.

Naturally, I was very nervous on our flight to Nyamlel in Trackmark's little Cessna Caravan. I remembered the threat made to Lady Cox that "we will shoot you out of the air" if caught flying into "no go" areas.

We were blasted with oppressive heat as we exited the aircraft in Nyamlel where I met for the first time the people whose lives had been altered forever by the slave raids in this area. They were facing much deprivation and even starvation. They greeted us warmly and unloaded the supplies and medicines we had brought and took them into town.

Caroline Cox talked with the commissioner of West Aweil County about what was going on in the area. The civilian administrators keep track of every person; they know who is missing, dead, or enslaved.

Walking through Nyamlel, I was appalled at the wreckage. Nyamlel was once the British Administrative Center and had been beautiful and well-developed. The NIF soldiers and Muslim militia rampaged through the town in 1995 and reduced it to rubble. The emotional impact was equally devastating; they killed eighty-two people and took 262 women and children as slaves.

The Sudan People's Liberation Army (SPLA) expressed total commitment to us because of CSI's consistent showing of care and concern. They said that when the last man had fallen, only then would we be on our own.

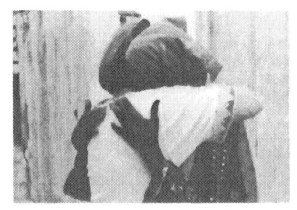

Lady Cox embraces
a woman who was freed
during an earlier trip.

I was on the spot I had
heard and read about. I
was loaded with cash and
watching a long line of
barefoot and bedraggled
men, women, and children
approach. These were
the people whose freedom
I had come to purchase!

Angelo, our chief
translator, approaches
the meeting place with
us. During the writing
of this book, Angelo's
village was raided and
his wife and children
were taken as slaves.
He was away doing
relief work at the time.

Boys and girls taken as slaves were often given the job of tending the animals, fetching water, and cleaning. It was not uncommon for them to receive beatings and to sleep outside in makeshift shelters or with the animals.

50,000 Sudanese pounds, packets the size of a pound of butter, were handed over for each slave as the redemption price. The money disappeared into the deep pockets of the white-robed slave traders.

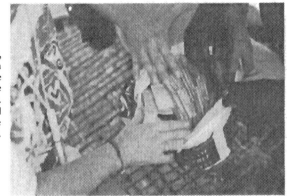

The slaves did not know that we were there to set them free. They sat patiently, stoically, with blank, emotionless expressions on their faces and lifeless eyes. Most of them were barefoot and dressed in rags.

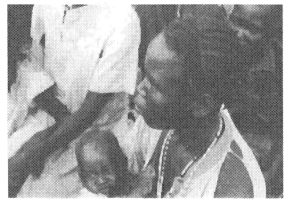

Many of the women were beaten and raped by their owners and used as concubines; some had children with Arab features, fathered by their captors.

Smiles broke out spontaneously after the slaves learned of their freedom. The preteen girls were probably the most vulnerable, and some of them were retrieved before they were to be circumcised.

This man spotted his wife and children in the long line of slaves then waited patiently through the long transaction before being reunited with them.

The slaves were almost starving. Many had reddish hair which is a sign of malnutrition. Some reported that all they had to eat was the leftovers; one woman ate the husks of the sorghum she had to grind. They were forced to work night and day.

This man received back his son but his wife is still missing. The slaves were beaten if they did not perform according to their masters' wishes. Many were made to convert to Islam.

Three young boys were rescued from slavery but their families were not located. The local chief took responsibility for them.

Lady Cox and John
Eibner greet Apin Apin
Akot. Mr. Akot sold
all he had to buy
back his family but
was at first only able
to rescue his wife
and younger daughter.

With CSI's assistance,
Mr. Akot was able to
make the dangerous trip
north again to redeem
his older daughter before
she was circumcised.
The scar is from being
slapped with a stick.

Lady Cox and Cal
Bombay meet periodically
with local commercial
traders to discuss peace
agreements between the
Dinka tribe and moderate
Muslims in the area.
Peacemaking is another
part of CSI's mission.

The people of Nyamlel still worship in their church damaged by mortar shelling.

Refugees crowd the towns of Kitgum fleeing the "Lord's Resistance Army." Encouraged and equipped by Khartoum, the army terrorizes the countryside, conscripting young boys for war fodder and enslaving girls to be used as concubines.

We wanted to travel the roads that would be used to transport food to see if they were passable.

The roads are extremely rough. It took us five hours to travel ninety miles. We thought we would be bounced right out of the car. This truck gave out on us.

🜨

chapter nine

FOOD AIDE

I have never been hungry. Not really! But I was deeply involved
with the relief operation during the great famine in Ethiopia.
Through the Emergency Response and Development Fund which I
administer, we spent almost 8 million dollars of Canadian money,
working together with the Canada Food Grains Bank which was
subsidized by the Canadian International Development Agency
(CIDA).

It had been my duty to travel to Ethiopia several times to meet
and make arrangements with the various people who would work
with us to ensure the helicopters we had hired would get the food
to the most inaccessible mountainous areas of Ethiopia. I accom-
panied the helicopters on several food deliveries. I saw things I
never want to see again.

I watched an Ethiopian father come out of a tent with his dead
child in his arms. Himself with emaciated arms and glistening
eyes, he wrapped the child in a piece of gauze-like white cloth,
and began the walk to the large open pit where more than fifty
people had been placed already that day—a common grave for
those who died in that refugee camp.

I watched an Ethiopian with the most unenviable responsibility imaginable. As people dragged themselves into a feeding station in wide open, dry country, he had to make a judgment call. There was not enough food to keep them all alive. He had to decide who was beyond help so that others could have food and live.

I learned that this same threat of death is now faced by hundreds of thousands of people in southern Sudan.

So on August 5, 1997, I found myself on a jet leaving Toronto bound for Ethiopia.

I had just finished teaching and preaching at Lakeshore Pentecostal Camp three days before. On the closing Saturday of my week there, I was asked to speak about the Sudan slavery "thing." The tabernacle was crowded.

Although no offering was taken during the service for the Sudan work of slave redemption or the feeding of those facing starvation, the district superintendent, Rev. Rick Hilsden, suggested that if people wanted some of my books or to help in the work I was doing in Sudan, they could see me at the back of the tabernacle. Mary and I were mobbed, and the total money that was handed to us within about twenty minutes was $9,750.

So there I was again at Pierson International Airport with a large wad of American cash bound around my waist in a fanny pack, a Sony DV1000 video camera, and a backpack ready for a hike into the part of Sudan where the Blue Nile flows, but where people were reported to be dying of starvation. Displaced and chased by the NIF and the GOS (Government of Sudan troops) they were trying not to be caught in the crossfire between the SPLA (their protectors) and the combined forces of the NIF and the PDF. Because of that, it was impossible to cultivate crops. They had no food and no place to get food.

I had arranged to meet John Eibner in Addis Ababa on August 7, hopefully at the airport. I had also agreed to John's suggestion that a man by the name of Bona Malwal come with us on this venture, since he is a man with many friends in high places, including friends in Ethiopia.

Bona Malwal's sister, who is a nurse, had been captured in a slave raid and taken north. She was among those who had been redeemed before I ever knew about the Sudan horrors.

Bona was the minister of information and culture in Sudan. For a time he was minister of industry in the cabinet of Numeiry in Sudan after Numeiry's earlier coup was legitimized by a democratic election. Bona was also the editor of the *Sudan Times,* the only English newspaper remaining after Sudan became independent from British rule in 1956.

Bona Malwal happened to be out of Sudan when Ahmed el Beshir staged his military coup in 1989. Beshir is still looking for the person who "tipped Bona off." There was no tip-off. Bona was merely out of the country on business. He now lives in London and is a Fellow at Oxford University.

Without knowing it, I flew into Addis Ababa on the same flight with Bona Malwal. We met when Arop Deng, an officer of the Sudan Relief and Rehabilitation Association (SRRA) met both of us inside the customs area in the Addis Airport. Arop was able to get us through the otherwise tedious and often frustrating procedures of entry into Ethiopia. Even though a new government is in power, the vestiges of communist harshness and authoritarianism still control the attitudes and actions of many of the civil servants.

Bona Malwal is a tall man as are most from the Dinka tribe in southern Sudan. There was instant rapport between us. John

Eibner was not at the airport. He had been delayed, along with Lady Cox, in getting out of the Beja area of Sudan where they had a harrowing experience while investigating the violations of human rights against the Beja people by the Khartoum-inspired soldiers.

Our plan was to approach the Minister of Foreign Affairs of the Ethiopian government to ask for permission to do a cross-the-border feeding program in the Blue Nile area of Sudan where there were reports of widespread starvation. We also wanted to go on the road which would be used to carry the grain, since we heard it was impassable, and we wanted to be sure that it could indeed be used for our purposes. Again, this would be a covert operation— one the leaders of the National Islamic Front (NIF) would never condone.

The SPLA had won a series of victories on the ground, driving out the forces of the NIF, but the civilian population was severely disrupted. They had been unable to plant crops for about two years. Antonov bombers would fly over and drop bombs indiscriminately on civilians. I had been told that about 50,000 had fled into Ethiopia just a few miles from the Sudan border and were in refugee camps being fed by United Nations agencies. But many hundreds of thousands more were reluctant to leave their homes and land for the dubious privilege of living in cramped refugee camps.

I made contact with Don Raymer, a personal friend and a representative of the Canada Food Grains Bank, before I left Canada. He gave me the name of their representative in Ethiopia, Mr. Sam Vander Ende. I got him on the phone in Addis just as he was packing to return to Canada for a six-week furlough. I told him what we wanted to do, and he said, "If you get permission to do a cross-border feeding program, I'll tip my hat to you!" Apparently, others had tried and failed.

Meanwhile Bona Malwal was making a few courtesy calls from the Imperial Hotel where we had all checked in. The hotel was "imperial" in name only.

Bona also phoned his friend Seyoum Mesfin, Minister of Foreign Affairs in Ethiopia, to set up an appointment. Mr. Mesfin was expecting us since Bona had talked with him just a few days before, outlining the basics of what we would like to do. Minister Mesfin agreed to meet us late on the Friday we were to be in Addis Ababa.

As we entered the compound of the ministry building we were frisked and had to surrender our passports, something I'm not altogether comfortable in doing when I'm outside Canada. We were escorted to the waiting room of the minister. We waited.

And we waited some more. Someone came and served us tea. And we waited.

Finally, we were ushered into the office of the minister. It was obvious that Bona and the minister were old friends. Yemane Kidane, the chief of the minister's cabinet joined us. Bona made introductions all round. There was a warmth about these two men that was quite attractive.

We sat and sipped a fresh supply of sweet tea. When I was introduced to the minister, it was mentioned that I had been involved in feeding the hungry in Ethiopia during the famine, especially in the canyon areas back in the 1980s.

The atmosphere was very warm and cordial. Within a few minutes, we had been given verbal permission to implement the feeding program. We then mentioned that we'd like to cross into

Sudan the next evening. This presented a few problems since the minister in charge of national security would have to be involved, and the local Ethiopian authorities on the border with Sudan also had a degree of authority which could block our going in.

Yemane Kidane left immediately to start making telephone calls. We left the office with the assurance that they would do what they could. Considering that it was late on a Friday evening, there didn't seem like there was much they could do. Most government offices were already closed.

Meanwhile, we booked a domestic flight to the town closest to the border, Asosa, from where we would try to cross into Sudan. Finding a return flight was a problem. We would have to charter a special plane to get us back to Addis Ababa.

Our flight to Asosa was the next day, so we spent another night at the Imperial Hotel. Bona Malwal invited another officer of the SRRA to join us for dinner that evening, Dr. Manywiir Arop. He was introduced as the medical officer for the SRRA. It was an eye-opening conversation. A novice in these things, I sat with these men and heard all the convoluted politics involved in the relationships between Ethiopia and Sudan. I also learned of the various factions within southern Sudan who were sometimes in unity and at other times at odds with each other. Their one point of unity was in fighting off the violations of their people by the Khartoum regime.

It dawned on me that Dr. Arop was the man from whom I needed to get a letter. I wanted to get donations of medicines for the civilian population of southern Sudan. The pharmaceutical companies in Canada had to have assurances that the medicines could, and indeed *would* be sent into Sudan and would be administered by qualified personnel. Dr. Arop was able to give me the letter I needed. Things were clicking into place.

I had no idea what I was to face the next day.

Bona Malwal, John Eibner, and I were driven out to the airport in Arop Deng's rickety old car. Getting through security was an experience long to be remembered. My video camera with its batteries and charger passed through the X-ray and no questions were asked. A little flashlight on my belt and my Swiss army knife were another matter. They confiscated the knife, which was understandable, but also took the small batteries from my flashlight.

There were about fifteen people on this small domestic flight. As we were led out to the plane across the tarmac, we were suddenly approached by three men dressed in casual clothes who began to frisk us without even introducing themselves. Bona Malwal took great exception to this, demanding to know who they were. They said they were security officers, but offered no proof. Bona gave them a lecture on how they were ruining any tourist industry they might hope to have by their peremptory and rude approach. I was grinning like a Cheshire cat through it all. Obviously, Bona was a man who believed in human rights!

When we finally were permitted on board we taxied out to the runway, but a very scary shuddering enveloped the plane. The pilot turned back. We were escorted back into the terminal. Two hours later we were led out to the plane again. The front landing wheel on the plane had been replaced.

Although we had been watched from the time we got off the plane, they insisted on frisking us again—even though they still had my knife and batteries (which were returned to me when we finally landed in Asosa).

Bona was deeply annoyed at this second search. He again lectured them soundly on how to win or lose tourists.

It was one of the more notable flights of my life. We had three stops on the way to Asosa.

It was the rainy season. The first stop was at a town with a dirt airstrip. As it turned out, it was a mud airstrip. We landed anyway—holding our breath. The next stop just seemed to be on the top of a hill, no airstrip in sight. We landed on a wide strip of grass in an open field. Several passengers got off and a Landrover came chugging up over the edge of the hill to carry them away. There was a flag on a pole, a little tin shack, and several forty-four-gallon drums with a hand pump. They refueled while we wandered over to the edge of the bush and tended to our own business.

With grass slapping the wheels, we took off again, this time for Asosa. It was hills and fog all the way, but through the breaks in the fog, the country looked lush and productive. When we landed at Asosa it was mud again. Lots of mud. A four-wheel-drive Toyota was there to pick us up, and we headed into the town of Asosa on a slick and muddy raised road. The driver had problems keeping the vehicle on the crown of the road, and eventually he lost. The front left wheel dropped into a large hole where the road had eroded, and the back right wheel went up into the air, spinning uselessly.

One of the reasons we wanted to go into Sudan was to see if the roads were passable. If trucks were unable to get through these roads, we had a problem. Although we had been told, "No problem," I was beginning to have my doubts.

This was the main road from Addis Ababa to this western part of Ethiopia. So, with our assurances of "no problem" we set out on foot, slipping and sliding our way into the small but busy little town of Asosa. We were led into the compound of a "hotel" where we were to take refreshments while a huge four-wheel-drive truck was sent back to haul our vehicle out of the hole.

Once inside the "hotel" compound, we ordered food. I should say Bona ordered the food. It was a grayish looking pancake that was cold. Various odd little piles of other things ringed the gray stuff. The idea was to take some of the gray stuff and use it to pick up the surrounding foods. I recognized some potatoes, so I tried them. Not bad. I tried something else and thought I had put flames in my mouth. We were served the ever-present Coca Cola.

Finally our Toyota arrived. I got a better look at it. No license plates. A SPLA flag on the windshield. And a number of guns mixed in with our camping gear. I was given the privilege of sitting in the cab with the driver and Bona Malwal. There was a light rain, lubricating the road even more. But John Eibner chose to sit in the open back of the vehicle. I offered to spell him off for a while, but he wouldn't hear of it. My legs were somewhat shorter that Bona's so I sat in the middle, where my left knee kept getting hammered as the driver changed gears. After the first few miles, I turned to find what was digging into my back. Another rifle. They kindly shifted it, and I was somewhat more comfortable. Three SPLA soldiers and a young mechanic were in the back with John.

Our first stop was at a junction not too far outside Asosa. We were to take the road leading to the Sudan border and therefore we were suspect. There were a few soldiers with rifles, yet it all seemed rather casual. A young man approached the window and engaged me in conversation. He said he was a schoolteacher, but began to ask where I was going. I evaded the question which was repeated several times in several different ways. Then he asked if I knew Malik Agar. Since I had never met him, I was able to honestly answer no. He then asked me again where I was going. Finally I said, "Wherever this Toyota goes, I'm going." He nodded with a knowing grin and walked off.

About all I knew about Malik Agar was that he was a commander in the SPLA somewhere inside Sudan.

Time was running along, and we were just sitting. Bona, John, and I decided to walk ahead to where some women were selling mangoes and bananas on the road. Someone shouted at us, warning us not to pass a certain tree up ahead. We bought some bananas and mangoes. Delicious. We bought extra to take along.

Finally, someone, somewhere agreed with someone else, and we were on our way.

I never worked so hard in my life to simply sit down. It was only ninety miles, but it took more than five hours to get to the Sudan border. The roads were a mess. On the hills, rocks and erosion made the road a hazard. In the low areas, mud was axle deep and interlaced with tree branches sometimes four inches in diameter. Great gouts of mud occasionally splashed forward then backward onto the windshield. The rain stopped and started again. The three-quarter-ton Toyota took it all in stride—and slide. The driver had obviously done this a few times before.

They assured me the large, all-wheel-drive trucks had an easier job of it. Looking at the large tire tracks in the chewed up road, I thought perhaps they were right. Several such trucks passed us coming from the other direction. That took some pretty neat maneuvering.

I asked them to stop at one point so I could get pictures of a massive refugee camp off to the left side of the road. It was made up of hundreds of grass-roofed mud huts. I was told that people were reluctant to come to the camps since it usually took weeks to establish that they were indeed refugees from Sudan and were given no rations until the process was complete. Meanwhile, they lived off what they could get from sympathetic refugees who already had status, and thus, food. It seemed even more urgent to me that food be delivered *into* Sudan so that the people could stay on their own land and be ready when the next planting season arrived.

These roads were treacherous. On the way we saw two of the large trucks off the road, one of them upside down. We were told that nine Ethiopian soldiers had been killed when it slid off the road and overturned. We passed an army tank with its turret pointed down the road in the direction we were going. I looked back a few times until we were out of range.

Several times we got stuck and had to walk ahead, slipping and sliding while the driver and passers-by pushed and pulled the truck back into a position where it could get traction—it was sometimes right off the road and turned sideways to climb a bank. I was amazed at their ability to force that truck through anything.

While we were still inside Ethiopia, I saw soldiers, both alone and in groups and well armed, casually walking down the road or sitting with rifles slung over their shoulders.

As we bounced and slid over rocks on the hill and mud holes filled with tree branches on the flat stretches or in the valleys, I marveled at the rich vegetation. Ethiopian people had maize (white corn) growing on hillsides and in clearings all along the road. It was just about a foot high and far from harvest, but looked lush. Because of the rough ride, however, I was getting a cramp in my right arm from holding onto the dashboard.

Hours later, as we rounded a bend on the top of a hill, the driver suddenly showed excitement and pointed down across a long valley and said one word, "Kurmuk." I didn't see anything. We got closer on another rise, and again, with even more enthusiasm, he pointed and said "Kurmuk." I thought I saw a flash of reflected light from the setting sun. But what did one tin roof signify?

My arms and back were aching by the time we finally got to the border. And what a strange border it was.

It was guarded by a single Ethiopian soldier with a rifle. The border crossing consisted of two thin poles stuck in the ground, one on each side of the road, with a single piece of string looped from one side to the other. The gun seemed to be a little more of a deterrent than the string. But it was a nice string—half of it was red.

The soldier ambled over, asked for our passports, and said we couldn't pass without permission. Permission. Who was authorized to give us permission? Amiable conversation and some laughter was exchanged. It became apparent that at this border they were used to SPLA people going back and forth. Everyone seemed to know everyone. Finally the soldier grinned and waved us through.

§

chapter ten

KURMUK

The string was untied, and we were in Sudan. It was then that I discovered we were in a vehicle which had been captured from the NIF some months before. One, apparently, of many.

We were told that we would meet Commander Malik Agar just a short distance ahead. The sun was setting and because of the terrible condition of the road, we were delayed several hours. We dipped down through what was at that moment a dry sandy creek bed then bounced up the other side. The driver, who had been quiet through most of the trip, said, "We have arrived." All I could see were trees through the dusk, which comes quickly near the equator.

Then we rounded a bend in the road, and suddenly we were in a large town. There were no lights anywhere. Darkness settled upon us as we pulled up and bounced to a stop under a large tree with roots spreading out for ten feet across the top of the ground.

I was stiff and sore. John Eibner and Bona Malwal crawled off the back of the pickup and didn't seem to be in much better condition. We all stretched and groaned. John admitted to being scared he would be bounced right out of the pickup several times. The soldiers seemed so used to it that you'd think they had just stood up after sitting in an easy chair.

We were greeted by several men in casual but well-worn clothes and were taken into a building where a mosquito net was hanging over a bed in the central breezeway. In a side room, a table with a dozen chairs—only some of them with intact backs—stood around a small table. Several kerosene lamps were brought in and put on the small table. We all sat in the lamp-lit gloom.

A broad shouldered man in battle fatigues walked into the room. Everyone quickly got to their feet. This was the legendary Malik Agar. Then another taller man came in. He was obviously a Dinka and very dignified. This was not Dinka country. The local people were much more broad shouldered. We were introduced to Commander Malik Agar. He was told I was a Canadian. He looked me in the eyes for some time, quietly, as though he were assessing me.

Malik Agar seemed to know John from a former visit. The commander was an impressive figure. We shook hands all round. There were about ten people in the room. The taller, older man from Dinka country in Bahr el Ghazal was introduced to us. He was the former Sudan ambassador to London, England—in better times. His name was Philip Obeng, and he had a cheerful smile on his seventy-year-old face.

We sat down again, and Philip Obeng told us that although he was from Dinka country, when he heard that Kurmuk had fallen to the SPLA, he came to see the town. He said he found it a most wonderful and peaceful place and had decided that he would settle here until his death. He seemed very much at peace with everyone and everything around us.

Conversation began, and it wasn't long before Commander Agar began to tell the history of his victories in the Blue Nile state.

He told of taking the town the first time without too much trouble or resistance from the NIF/GOS forces. They had captured a good quantity of ammunition and several large trucks. Then the town had been shelled and attacked and was retaken from the SPLA. He readily admitted, with a certain amount of chagrin, the tactical mistakes he had made. But he also made it clear that no defeat from the NIF is final.

He strengthened his fighting force and using the weapons and ammunition he had captured the first time, he retook the town. He said, "They will not get it back now, because I control the whole area now." In fact, he controlled an area larger than the U.K.

Then with grim face, he told how he came close to capturing several tanks, but that they "outsmarted me this time."

As soon as Kurmuk was secure, he turned his attention to a gold mine twenty kilometers away and operated under the Chinese. There were forty Chinese on the site. When he attacked the gold mine, he expected to capture them as well. They surprised him by taking flight over the top of a nearby mountain. He said, "I didn't think they'd be strong enough to climb the mountain..."

When he got the records of the mine, Malik said they showed that over 10 million dollars worth of gold had been mined already, but he was of the opinion that there was probably more than that shipped out. He occupied the mine, shutting it down for the time being. All the machinery in the mine had Chinese script on the switches, gauges, and dials, etc.

He described the opulence of the residences of the Chinese compared to the hovels of the African workers in the mine. He looked at me and hinted that perhaps a Canadian company might want to operate the mine. I answered a noncommittal, "Perhaps."

He offered to take us out to see the mine the next morning. We said we would if we had time, since our plan was to return to Ethiopia the next day—again by road. We had a plane to catch in Asosa.

I asked, "Aren't you afraid of being bombed?"

He smiled a broad smile and said, "They won't come this close to the Ethiopian border with bombers. There are antiaircraft installations just over that hill." He pointed behind me in the dark room. "In Ethiopia," he added, "they won't let a Sudanese aircraft come this close to their border." Kurmuk is almost right *on* the border.

While we were talking, to my surprise a white man with an obvious American accent walked into the room, but was not introduced. He sat in a chair to my left and tried to engage me in conversation. I was puzzled by his presence, but too interested in what the commander was saying to listen to him at that point. I noted only that he had an obviously American accent.

Malik Agar went on talking about some of his actions against the NIF. Then he brought up the fact that he had forced Chevron to leave the oil field they were developing. He said he could not allow the government in Khartoum to have that developed, since they would use the money to annihilate the black people of the south.

He said, as he kept glancing at me, "I warned the Americans four times to get out and to shut down the oil field, but they wouldn't listen. I didn't want to kill Americans." Finally he attacked and during the attack, four Americans were killed. He said, "Chevron shut down the whole operation and left."

Someone came into the room with a large bowl, a pitcher of

water, and a bar of soap. I knew from my seventeen years in Kenya that food was coming. They handed the bar of soap to each one in turn, poured water over our hands into the bowl, then rinsed them again after we had soaped thoroughly. It's a healthy way to start a meal. They don't do that even at the Sheraton!

We were all invited out into the large hallway where the bed had been and where now a table was spread with food. Some of it I recognized. Fresh-baked bread, goat meat, and thin sorghum pancakes. There were potatoes, vegetables, and gravy to dip the food and bread into. It was delicious. Other things I did not recognize, but ate them anyway. While we were eating, the American introduced himself to me as Tim Eckland, saying that he was in the "scrap metal" business. He claimed he wanted to truck out spent shell casings. "For recycling," he said. He puzzled me.

When he found out we were there to make arrangements to truck food in to the starving civilian population, he tried to strike a deal. He had the best prices you could find in Addis Ababa. We could ship the food in on the same trucks he would use to ship the brass casing out. He handed me a business card, which, knowing he was American, seemed to me like a very substandard card. It had the name of some "consultants" company on it. It had an address in Cairo, Egypt. He wrote an American telephone number on it which would get to him wherever he was in the world. I felt very uneasy about him. John Eibner, himself an American citizen, whispered in my ear later that he was feeling uneasy about "this fellow Tim." He might be something else entirely. Somehow I could not imagine 250 truckloads of spent shells going out of Kurmuk, since that was the number of truckloads we were planning to ship in for a start.

Commander Agar told me he would set aside four of his trucks to pick up the food at the border. He went on to say, "Tomorrow morning you will probably see several hundred people who will come here for food and medicine. We don't have enough to give them. We try to convince them to cross over to Ethiopia to the refugee camps where there is food. They don't want to leave their land. It's a tough problem" he added.

I found out later that he had been appointed by the SPLA as governor of the Blue Nile area as well as commander of the SPLA. That made him responsible for the civilian population as well as the military. I also found out he was the only university graduate from that whole area. He had been educated in Khartoum, and was always under the impression that he was an Arab. Yet he was black. Since this area was predominantly Muslim, he had simply assumed he was an Arab because all his schooling was in Arabic, and no one ever told him anything different. I asked him what his religion was. With a grin he said, "I am a reluctant Muslim."

He has nine brothers and sisters, and three of them had become Christians in recent months. He was going "to church" himself occasionally.

While we were eating, Bona Malwal talked with the commander and the former ambassador for some time. Bona is the editor of an eight-to-twelve-page publication called the *Sudan Gazette* which he publishes out of England. I later read in the *Gazette* some of what he had learned from Malik Agar, most of which Bona told me on our return to Ethiopia.

When the meal was over, Commander Agar approached me and recalled his statements regarding the Chevron oil installation. He then said, "There is a Canadian company now developing an oil field just up north of here. As soon as the chairman (meaning Dr. John Garang, the head of the SPLA armies) gives me the word, I am going to attack and destroy that installation." Then he just looked at me. Finally he added, "There are Canadians there, and I do not want to see any Canadians killed."

Then he added, "It is just a seven-hour march from the area I control."

I think I got the unspoken message—"Warn your government!"

With that, I was beginning to wonder why I couldn't be satisfied with simply staying in Canada, doing my daily Bible teaching commentaries on *100 Huntley Street,* and safely going home to feed my chickens every night? How did I get in this deep? And who *was* this Tim Eckland, really?

We discussed what we would do tomorrow, and the Commander reiterated his commitment to supply four trucks to get food into the civilians. He asked only that we send a barrel of fuel with each truckload to deliver the food. That was reasonable.

We were led to various buildings in Kurmuk to bed down for the night—and there actually was a bed. I was given a room in a damaged house, but which had an ingenious latrine in the back courtyard. It also had great gaping holes in rusty old screens in the door and windows. John Eibner pitched his tent in the courtyard under a tree, his tent was mosquito-proof. I have no idea where Bona Malwal slept. Tim Eckland had said good night and had drifted off into the darkened town.

I awakened to the sound of "hut hut hut" as a large group of soldiers ran past in perfect formation, dressed in boots, camouflage, and not-quite-white undershirts. I got my first look at

Kurmuk in daylight. It was much larger than I had imagined. I quickly dressed, ate some canned food I had brought, drank a liter of water, packed my kit and carried it up to the Commander's place where we had talked and eaten the night before.

I set up my video camera for an interview with Malik Agar. He told of the youngsters, which the NIF had conscripted into their army, and how that they had all been given little booklets with quotations from the Koran about paradise, together with a "key to heaven."

These were supposedly reminders that what they were doing was worth any risk because dying on the battlefield for the jihad meant automatic entry into paradise. The key was supposed to be used to open the door to paradise should they be killed in action.

Malik said this was simply a ruse to deceive these child soldiers. From those he captured he learned that their training was two weeks long, and they shot one bullet at a target before they were sent to fight the SPLA.

Talking with Commander Malik Agar again later, I asked him about his army. Since most of the SPLA in the Bahr el Ghazal area were Christians, I assumed this was also the case in the Blue Nile area. He told me that 90 percent of his army was Muslim. That is, they were Muslims who would neither bow to the radical fundamentalism of the Khartoum government, nor allow themselves to be Arabic.

He told me the other 10 percent were Christians or animists.

I remembered the CBC reporter who tried to squeeze me into saying that what I had been doing was simply pitting Christians against Muslims. This blew that theory out the window. These were *Muslims* fighting against a radical fundamentalist Muslim government.

Somewhere in our conversation, Commander Malik Agar asked if I could send him something to read. He wanted to have books. I told him I would, and when I returned I sent him some, including my last book, *A View From The Barn.*

Commander Agar had a bodyguard gathered to escort us as he showed us through the town of Kurmuk. The town was somewhat of a shambles, but it's former beauty and tranquillity in these lush hills was still evident. I could see why the former ambassador would want to settle down in such a tranquil place.

But, buildings were now pockmarked from shells and mortars. Some buildings were ruined. Malik showed where, as he put it, the NIF had "desecrated the church, and turned it into a mess hall for its officers." He seemed deeply offended by what they had done to the church property and the mission houses.

He took us through the town square, where a few businesses were beginning to open up again.

As we circuited through the town, he showed us the civil government buildings which were now being repaired. It was quite impressive. All the while, armed SPLA soldiers spread out in front, around and behind us as we walked. He showed us another area where he had some tanker trucks, and a number of other trucks he had captured from the NIF. "We don't keep many here," he said. Some were being repaired.

At one point we came to a place where a thirteen-year-old girl was standing in a mud hole beside a building with a pan in her hand. I asked the Commander what she was doing. He smiled and said, "She's panning for gold." I asked if they got much. He said, "Enough to survive."

Then he took us to another, smaller place enclosed on three

sides by buildings and with several massive trees in the middle. It was crowded with people, some in rags, some children with no clothes at all. Every one of them was thin, many with bloated stomachs. Here stood the reasons I had come to this place.

The Commander said, "These are the ones we will have to turn away today. Every day it is like this. People looking for food. People come back to town now that they know it's safe. They need food. They need seed. They need everything."

Through interpreters, we talked to them. They told us that they were searching for food. With nothing growing on their land and the fear of high-level bombing, whole families were on the move; they fled to this town close to the Ethiopian border. Word had spread. Kurmuk was safe. The SPLA controlled it.

All they wanted was food, and all we had were a few candies. We gave them what we had. I began to wish the impossible, that we had brought a truck of maize with us. But that would take time. Meanwhile I was looking into the faces, and worse still, into the eyes of people who had no idea where their next mouthful of food would come from, if it came at all.

It's an awful feeling to be helpless in the face of such need.

Some of these people were dressed in fine clothes, and the women and girls had the most ornate styles woven into their hair. Some wore bright and lively colors, but there faces reflected nothing but hopelessness. I took 35mm pictures. Some of their arms were as thin as broomsticks. I felt sick.

With a heavy heart, I went back with the others to where the Toyota was and where Commander Malik Agar had camped in town for the night we were there. We prepared to leave. Tim Eckland hovered around and finally said good-bye to us, even though the evening before he had decided to return to Ethiopia with us. It's not every day a ride is available out of Kurmuk—to anywhere! I was left with a lot of questions about the man.

I had a multiple-entry visa to go to Ethiopia, knowing that I would be in and out and in again. It was time to go, and it was almost comical. This time we were going to use two trucks. One started with the battery. The other was started with about ten men pushing it until it kicked into life. You use what you have, I guess. They put me in the truck with the starter. John and Bona opted for the one with the larger cab, but which needed a push start.

Unlike the day before, which was a mixture of rain, fog, and slick roads, it looked like a much better day. Perhaps the roads would be better. Perhaps it would not rain.

With our backpacks in the beds of the trucks, and a half dozen men with guns as well, we started for the border nearby. When we pulled up at the string across the road, an Ethiopian border guard approached the two Toyotas. We sat while the first driver talked with the guard. The soldier walked away. Local authority was being exercised.

The driver told us that we might as well get out and walk around, or sit under the tree. I offered to show my passport with the extra entry permit, but Bona Malwal advised me not to. So we waited.

A small group of people began to gather, everyone talking at once. The guard had a stern look on his face. It was a different guard than the one who had let us in the evening before. Now it was about twelve noon, and we had at least a five-hour drive ahead—if we got through...and the sun sets at about 7:15 P.M. We had a chartered flight waiting for us in Asosa, since there were no regular commercial flights on Sunday. I always seem to plan to leave Sudan on a Sunday!

Finally one of Malik Agar's soldiers suggested the guard send for someone who was in charge of the border. A young man was sent running. Perhaps a half hour later, a well-dressed man with a clipboard and glasses came ambling toward us. We watched. I was getting nervous. Bona must have noticed, and he said to me, "Don't worry, the guard is just trying to exhibit his authority. We'll get through."

Our driver and one of Malik Agar's soldiers hunkered down on their heels with the man at the side of the road and had a ten-minute conversation. The official waved the guard over, said something to him, and spoke to us, "Go ahead." Apparently the man with glasses and clipboard had been in radio contact with Addis Ababa. The guard officially took down the string, and we passed the two branches stuck in the ground and were once again in Ethiopia.

The ride back to Asosa was just as rough as the ride into Sudan, but the rain held off and we made much better time. The push-start Toyota overheated twice and finally gave up the ghost. A few stayed with the vehicle and the rest piled into the back of the Toyota I was in. At least it gave us better traction. On the way to Asosa, we picked up a few Ethiopian soldiers who needed to get a few miles down the road to relieve some others on point duty. This Toyota began to pant pretty heavily when we came to hills, but the driver was an expert. He stopped occasionally to pour water into the radiator.

When we got to Asosa, we went directly to the grass landing strip, and to our relief, the plane was waiting for us. The sun was out now, and as we loaded our stuff into the hold, climbed into the plane and sat down, we all heaved a great sigh of relief. We were starting the first leg of the return journey.

We flew over an area near Addis Ababa which looked severely flooded, with tin roofs standing out in the fields of water as the sun set. Africa, either dusty, dry, and hot or flooded beyond enough. Brown or green. Feast or famine. We had just faced famine.

When we got back to the Imperial Hotel for that night, it felt a little more imperial than it did the first few nights.

When we came down for a meal together before we all went to bed, I was walking past the entrance to the hotel where a guard frisked almost everyone who came in, and I heard my name called as if a question, "Cal Bombay?" I turned, and a white man with a baby in his arms asked if I was Cal Bombay. When I assured him that I was, the first thing he said to me was, "I went to college with your daughter, Elaine." I was flabbergasted. Who was this guy and these people with him? It turned out to be Darren Gingras, a P.A.O.C. missionary with his wife and a Scandinavian missionary couple who were "out on the town" with their small children. The Imperial served great pizza apparently.

We spent some time together, and when Bona and John came down to eat, I joined them after introductions. I didn't want to miss a part of my education on matters which might affect my involvement in the feeding program we had in mind. John left for Switzerland on an evening flight. I was booked out the next day.

I flew Ethiopian Airways to Frankfurt, then the next morning flew Lufthansa to Toronto.

It was wonderful to arrive home, and I hoped for a few days

off. I wanted to give some attention to Mary first of all. I also wanted to get at my vegetable gardens. Weeds were everywhere. Mary had, as usual, cared for all the animals—chickens, goats, cats, and dogs with her usual aplomb. All was well. Except me, perhaps, I was bushed.

I discussed my trip with David Mainse, president of CCCI and Fred Vanstone, chief of staff. I asked their advice on whether I should talk to Ottawa about what I had learned in Sudan. They felt that, since Canadian lives were possibly in danger, I should go to Ottawa. I also felt I had a duty to inform the Ministry of Foreign Affairs. Fortunately, I already knew the man I had to see.

The former secretary of state for Africa had said, "Our hands are tied." What would David say?

I telephoned David Kilgour, MP for Edmonton East and Secretary of State for Africa and Latin America and made an appointment. I flew to Ottawa and took a taxi to his office, arriving just fifteen minutes before the appointed time. David was a little late, and he and his wife had track suits on when they came into his office. I assumed they had gone out for a healthy jog during the lunch break. David told me with a grin, "No, we have just come from teaching in a DVBS." That's *my* kind of MP. DVBS is Daily Vacation Bible School—usually held for youngsters during the summer holidays.

David called in two of his assistants, Shig Uyeyama, the man on Canada's desk for Somalia, Ethiopia, and Sudan, and another lady who sat and said little, but wrote a lot. I told all, including the threat to Canadian lives. Coincidentally, or perhaps not, someone came into the office while I was there telling of this threat to report that a Canadian had been shot and wounded in the foot that same day—in Sudan. The next day it was in the papers and simply blamed on some unknown bandit. Not too many people believe that.

It's time the Canadian government took a strong stand on the human rights issues in Sudan. The west has paid attention to other atrocities throughout the world, but has remained mysteriously silent in regard to Sudan. And all this *in spite* of the well-documented accounts of atrocities by many different agencies, including the United Nations.

Thirty lives in jeopardy in some parts of the world hits the front pages around the world.

"Diplomacy" fuddles on while thousands remain in slavery and many more thousands face almost certain death by starvation.

◉

chapter eleven

REDEEMING
MORE SLAVES

I'd said, "I won't go back!" I'm still overweight and still getting older. I really wasn't anxious to go back to Sudan into the "no go" areas. It was tough slogging, and I'm simply not that tough. I said it a number of times, more to convince myself than anyone else. But how do you fight your own heart?

We had received more designated funds for the redemption of slaves in Sudan, so there was no question as to what the money had to be spent on. Designated funds go where they are designated. It was just *me* that didn't necessarily want to go where they were designated.

I had been receiving requests from a variety of journalists, asking that, if I was going again, could they go with me. My usual answer was, "I'll get back to you." There were certainly more requests to go than there were places on the small plane, particularly if we were going to take all the medical supplies we hoped to take.

I faxed and e-mailed back and forth with both John Eibner and Caroline Cox about another trip. We found a date that was available to all of us, settling on October 6–17.

I finally settled on the two journalists I felt comfortable in taking from Canada. One of them had come all the way down from Montreal to meet me and really pressed me to let him come along. His name is Pierre Richard. I felt good that a French newspaper in Canada would be represented. I put only two conditions on it— they had to pay their own way, and they had to contribute two thousand dollars toward the redemption of slaves. Pierre agreed to this.

This time I was going with no doubts at all about the fact that slavery on a massive scale was being fully condoned by the rogues who violently overthrew the Sudan government in 1989. They have ruled with the gun ever since. And to doubt the fact that they encouraged slavery in Sudan was impossible after listening to the slaves themselves. It has been estimated that there are tens of thousands of slaves still in bondage.

The *Calgary Sun* had a correspondent who had been in a lot of hot spots around the world, Linda Slobodian, and she also had been asking to come along. I described the conditions she would face and told her she would have to fork over two thousand dollars to help purchase the redemption of slaves. After she talked with her editor and after several telephone conversations, it was decided she would come along.

I arranged to meet John and Caroline at the airport in London. Linda would join my flight out of Toronto, and Pierre would go straight from Montreal to meet us in London.

My wife, Mary, was not really excited about this trip, particularly after hearing all that had happened on my first trip. She was afraid for my life, and I must admit, I had a few palpitations myself. I was much more aware of what I was facing this time, and that made it an even more daunting decision. There are times when ignorance is, if not bliss, well, it is ignorance! This time I was not ignorant about what I was facing. John Eibner had warned me, since it was the rainy season, to expect the possibility of wading through deep water at spots, "Up to at least your waist, or higher," he said. He had to do that on one of his treks in Bahr el Ghazal.

Mary voiced her trepidation several times, and I tried to assure her that everything would be fine. I knew there were a large number of people praying for me and for the others, but they didn't know *when* I was going. It's just not something you announce in advance, especially when some people just don't like you and would rather you be dead than reveal to the world the atrocities of slavery as it is practiced in Sudan.

Just days before I left, one of the students in our school of broadcasting, Richard Friedon, a Messianic Jew, came to me with a quiet excitement. He said, "I was praying for you last night, and I believe the Lord showed me a promise specifically for you." I'd had people approach me with "messages from the Lord" before, usually well intentioned. But I was ever-so-slightly skeptical—at first. He must have seen it in my eyes. But he became quietly insistent that I read a certain psalm. "It's for you," he kept repeating. After repeating the scriptural reference several times, I finally went up to my office and looked up Psalm 41:1–2. It says:

Blessed is he who considers the poor; The LORD will deliver him in time of trouble. The LORD will preserve him and keep him alive, and he will be blessed on the earth; you will not deliver him to the will of his enemies.

As I read it, my whole being was flooded with a totally inex-
plicable peace. The fears melted away. I shared it with Mary, but
I'm not too sure how much comfort *she* found in it. But for me, it
was total. And through the next few weeks, even months, until
this writing, that peace has been constant.

I should tell you that this particular chap who gave me this
promise from the Lord is a hard-nosed realist. He used to work
with Interpol. He's not unaware of the wretched realities in this
world in which we live. But he also knows the reality of God's
power and presence.

So, on October 6, 1997, I found myself again on my way to
the airport for another flight to London. I couldn't find Linda
Slobodian and thought perhaps she had backed out, although I
was certain she would have informed me. She seemed the type—
at least over the telephone.

When I checked in at the airport, the clerk said, "There's a
message here for you from a Ms. Slobodian." I wondered what was
coming. It turned out that she had simply caught an earlier flight
and would meet me at the airport in London. Good!

This time I was ready for the long flight. Caroline Cox had a
little inflatable pillow which wrapped around her neck and kept
her comfortable as she slept seated in the plane. Good idea. I
bought one, and it helped a lot. No stiff neck pain.

During the ten-hour stopover in London, I stayed in the same
hotel as Pierre. Linda also stayed there. I slept for a while, then
Pierre and I headed for the airport by way of Caroline Cox's office
where I did an interview with Caroline for the documentary we
would be producing.

At the airport we would meet up with John, and Linda. John

Eibner had asked me if it was all right for a Swiss journalist, Anton Christen, to come along as well. I had agreed. He was to meet us there as well.

When I walked into the departure hall, John Eibner was standing in the middle of the open concourse. Pierre and I walked up to him just as Caroline was coming from the other direction. Anton Christen came up from my left, and we were all introduced, then, just as I was wondering where Linda Slobodian had gone, she called to me as she was coming up an escalator to my right. Everything was clicking into place nicely. I hoped the rest of this venture would run as smoothly.

Just days before, John had called me and said the Cessna Caravan would not carry all the medicines and supplies we had to take into Sudan. Since the Emergency Response and Development Fund was paying for the costs of this trip, John asked me if I would be willing to pay the extra for a DC 3. After considering the load, medicines, and now people, I had little choice, and agreed, although it wasn't too much more costly. Anton Christen paid his own share of the flight into Sudan, which reduced it for the ERDF. If we were able to redeem as many slaves as we hoped, the average cost would still be slightly less than three hundred U.S. dollars per redeemed slave.

We checked in all our duffel bags of food, backpacks of personal stuff; and each of us, dressed down for the occasion in jeans, hiking boots, and day packs, headed for the plane. Caroline Cox was in jeans too, but she sported a pearl necklace throughout the whole trip. That, and her warm smile—always.

Sleep was fitful as it always is for me on a jet, but this time we landed at Kenyatta International Airport and went through customs and immigration. The big old refurbished DC 3 was out on the tarmac waiting for us. We wouldn't have to drive miles this time to get to Wilson Airport.

But there was some business to do. This time we were required to pay a visa charge for going into southern Sudan, controlled by the SPLA/SPLM. Dr. Justin Yaac met us at the airport, and we were given a private room in the domestic area of the airport to wash up, change, have a few bottles of cold pop, change U.S. dollars into Sudanese pounds, and generally get reoriented for the next leg of the journey.

Perhaps I should clarify the "price of a slave." The actual cash turned over to the slave traders was not the full three hundred dollars. This amount also covers other costs, such as the price of leasing the planes, war-risk insurance for the plane going into Sudan, army rations, thousands of dollars worth of medicines, and many other incidentals. All of these costs were a part of the "price of a slave." It followed therefore, that the more slaves we could redeem at one time, the average cost would be less.

This time, "Heather" the owner of TrackMark, the relief flight company, would fly us north to Lokichokio. The DC 3 is a lumbering old machine, but reliable. It was packed with the medicines we had ordered, as well as two, twenty-one speed bicycles I had asked my friend Don Matheny to purchase for me. I wasn't going to walk myself to death this time if I could help it.

There was also an additional passenger. I learned he was Commander Paul Malong and was going back to join his units after having a series of operations in Nairobi. In seven different battles he had been wounded nine times. They removed some bullets and shrapnel, but he still had a few pieces of metal in him. He was a big strapping fellow and not overly generous with words at that point. He looked me over pretty closely.

After a good meal brought to the DC 3 by the TrackMark people, we settled into the long flight north.

I began to wonder, as I looked at the two boxes holding the bicycles and spare tires and parts, if we would be able to assemble them on time when we landed. They were on top of dozens of boxes of medicines. The DC 3 lumbered on, and I thought about it being somewhat slower and larger as a target if a MIG fighter sighted us. I knew that Sudan had the second largest air force in Africa after South Africa.

We were hoping to land at a place called Marial Bai, but when we flew over it, the dirt runway was too wet. We landed at Nyamlel again, with only a bit of wet mud flying around. Again, we landed at dusk. It was too late for the big white plane to take off, so Heather slept in the plane and took off in the morning.

After all had been unloaded from the plane onto the heads and into the arms of scores of happy people, we headed for the town of Nyamlel. Angelo and others whom I had met the last time came up to me with broad smiles, greeting me with hugs and back slapping. Angelo said, "It's good to see you come back…not everyone comes back." Somewhere along the line they began calling me "Uncle Cal."

It had rained heavily the day before. We ended up in the "Nyamlel Hilton" again. It started to rain in a very heavy tropical downpour. Try pitching a tent in a flooding rain! It's not fun. Various thatched houses were designated for each person in which to pitch their tent. We all had individual small tents. Mosquitoes were alive and well. This was the rainy season. Malaria is a killer.

But I was determined not to take Larium unless I felt the symptoms of malaria. I would recognize them. I had malaria twenty years before, in Kenya.

It was at that point that I learned that Linda Slobodian had never been in Africa before nor had she ever been camping. And here she was not knowing which part of the tent pointed up. I think it was Pierre who finally helped her! Oh and it was then that we found out that she's scared senseless of spiders. We tried to reassure her—without lying. She sprayed enough bug killer to render *herself* unconscious.

I was having my own problems. I had chosen to stay at the "Nyamlel Hilton," rather than in a grass-roofed tukul. I would sleep inside the storage room, but because of the mosquitoes I had to put up my tent. I had a tin roof over my head and a cement floor at my feet. The tent was easy to put up, but with a little flashlight only, and a roof that leaked like a sieve, I might just as well have pitched my tent in a hollow outside. The floor had a natural hollow—right under my tent. It was a damp night...

Before we retired, we ate together in the breezeway where I had slept back in March. Try to hold a flashlight with your teeth, a can with your left hand, and use a can opener with your right. Try to do it, and keep clean, knowing that your next bath is several hot and sticky days away.

The heat wasn't quite so bad this time, perhaps only 110 degrees, but it was a damp heat with all the rain.

Morning didn't come soon enough. When it did, we found, or I should say, *didn't* find the drinking water we brought with us. It had been on the plane, but had not arrived with all our gear at the "Nyamlel Hilton." This caused us considerable concern, and we had to pump extra water immediately. The pumps removed everything both living and dead, except chemicals. Since there were no chemicals in the water it was perfectly pure—though awfully "flat" tasting.

The River Lol was in full flow, and we had to cross it. We met with a team of Kenyan relief workers from the International Rescue Committee. I surprised them by greeting and talking to them in Kiswahili. They had come to try to help the local people in training in good hygiene. They were camped out under a large grass-roofed hut in front of the "Nyamlel Hilton." We spent some time catching up on the local situation.

We met with formerly freed slaves, as well as the Commissioner Aleu Akechak, and Commander Paul Malong Awan brought us up to date on the military situation. Antonov bombers had attacked Nyamlel in June, fortunately killing no one. They knew that an offensive was planned against Nyamlel and a place called Raga, just west of Nyamlel. But the NIF was having trouble getting recruits from among the moderate Muslims since a visit from Mubarak el Fadhi el Mahdi last year and letters carried by CSI from Sadiq el Mahdi in March on our last visit. These letters encouraged the moderate Muslim population to reject the overtures of the Khartoum radicals and not to join in the raids.

We were also told that the government had conscripted 70,000 students in the north who had just finished high school. My contact in the Canadian Ministry of Foreign Affairs had told me the same thing, suggesting it was too dangerous to go at this point.

These conscripted students were told they could not receive their graduation certificates until they served in the army for three years. Therefore, those wanting to enter university, even if they had their high school diplomas, could not enroll until they had served in the army for three years. From what we heard, a minimal training was given to these conscripts who were sent to the front within a few weeks. War fodder. Many ran away.

The time came to start our long walk, again in the general direction of Manyiel where we had freed the slaves in March. I asked for the twenty-one speed bicycles I had brought on the plane. They had been unable to find the mechanic to put them together. My heart sank.

They did have some bicycles, but they were fully loaded with all our stuff and some of the medicines. These were loaded into a large white fiberglass canoe with the wheels in the center and the loads hanging dangerously close to the water. The bicycles and about eight people went across on the first load. The river was moving swiftly, so they worked their way upriver on our side, then with only two people paddling, they made a mad dash for a small beach on the far side. They may have done this just to prove to us that it could be done.

Then they returned for the main baggage—us. Lady Cox, John Eibner, Linda Slobodian, Pierre Richard, Anton Christen, and I piled into the tipsy canoe with our legs stretched across more bicycles which were loaded with tents, duffel bags and what water we had. It was a sobering moment if you stopped to think what was invisible, yet deadly, in that water.

We made it, of course, with me recording much of it for possible use on television. This time we took a different route altogether than the last time. We walked along the edge of the river for several miles on paths as narrow as eight inches and grass on both sides of us as high as six feet, green and growing. The rains had been good.

Eventually we turned away from the river onto sandy paths where we could see the tracks of the bicycles which had gone on before us. After several miles, John Eibner, Caroline Cox, and Anton Christen had gone far ahead. Pierre was just barely in sight. Linda was beginning to look gray and waxen. I had fallen back to stay with her. When I asked how she was doing, she looked at me with a bleak look and said, "I don't know if I can make it...I'm serious." We decided to stop for a while under a tree with several armed SPLA soldiers who were bringing up the rear guard. We sat on the roots of some strange tree, panting and sipping water.

We repeated this several times. Linda was looking seriously worn out. I was not too displeased with having to walk more slowly and rest more often myself. I was no Olympic speed walker! I was bushed too. As we sat there, I happened to glance over at two thorn trees over my right shoulder. Something had caught my attention. I called Linda's attention to it. There were about a hundred or more Malibou storks standing on the tops of the two trees, like great awkward flowers. Malibou storks are scavengers. I didn't want to think what may have been some of their recent pickings.

As we sat under the tree resting, a fellow rode up on a psychedelic-colored bicycle. It turned out to be one of the two, twenty-one speed bicycles I had brought. Whoopee! I said, "Linda, here's your chance." She refused and said something like, "I can't ride a bike. I haven't been on one for over four hundred years,"—something to that effect. At about the same time, three donkeys crossed on a path nearby. A young lad crossed the path right behind them with a fourth donkey.

I asked Linda if she had ever ridden a horse. Affirmative. "Well," I said, "wanna have a go…?" Affirmative. One of the escorts commandeered the donkey, and we hoisted Linda on its back. Off she went with a young fellow leading the donkey. I would have bent the donkey in half, but Linda is slightly built and a bit short.

I got on the twenty-one speed bike and took off, passing Linda with the remark, "See you later." Actually, I saw her sooner rather than later. We were well behind the main party, so I peddled on, changing gears when I had to go up a rise and coasting when I could. But it was still hot and tiring. I pulled up under a tree, sat, sipped water, and rested. Linda went flying by on the back rack of another bicycle. A tall fellow named Paul Nang Magok had come down the trail, found Linda on the donkey, and transferred her to the back of his bike after padding the rack over the back fender with a blanket. I winced as I saw that bike hitting bumps.

Paul, whom Linda began to call "St. Paul," called back, "We'll be the first there." He was probably right. I just didn't know where "there" was.

On my way, now alone with two rifle-toting Dinka, I had only myself to think about. Probably not the most inspiring food for thought.

I stopped under one tree where there were rows of logs mounted on short posts imbedded in the ground, backless benches. One of the men told me it was a school, except on Sunday when it was a church. As I was sitting on one of the logs resting and sipping water, a mother and a child of about four years of age came out of the surrounding bush. They stopped and the child stared at me with big brown eyes. No fear, just a steady stare. But what struck me most was the book the child was clutching to his chest. It was old and a bit tattered and the title was in English, *Holy Bible*. I took some video, then climbed back on my bike. Somewhere along the line, my escorts had gone off on a side trail, saying they'd catch up with me. They never did.

☉

chapter twelve

LOST!

I was lost. My best clue was to look for bike tracks in the sand.
Sometimes I had to dismount and inspect several divergent
paths before I found the tracks again. Here I was in the south of
Sudan, alone, with a psychedelic, but flashy twenty-one speed bike
flying down trails I had never seen before!

I had lots of time to think. In spite of the politics and civil war
in the area, I came to one simple conclusion. Except as the politics
and the various factions either impede or expedite my ability to
free the slaves, feed the starving, and get medicine to civilians, I
had little or no real interest whatsoever in the politics of the situation. I merely wanted to show Christian compassion to people in
an awful life-and-death situation. That kept me pedaling.

I finally came to a point where I didn't know where to turn. As
best I could, I pointed with a question on my face. People pointed
me down one path, then another. After a long time I came to a
wide open space where there were several hundred men, women,
and children. It was some kind of community meeting. They
stared at me as though I was from outer space. No wonder—a
white man, with a video camera and wildly-colored, brand-new

bicycle. Every other bike in the county was black and broken in at least two places.

A fellow came over to me and greeted me. "I thought this was the place where the slaves would be set free," I said. "Not here," he answered. I was apparently several miles out of my way. A direction was suggested as the man pointed across an open plain of dried grass and some mango trees, and he said, "Perhaps you should go over there..." The "perhaps" bothered me a bit. I was not into "perhaps." I wanted to *know!*

What choice did I have? I had to find "those other white people." After a lot of water, several more stops, and a lot of peddling, I found an SPLA commander's camp, and sure enough, the whole gang was there.

Akot Deng Deng Akot was the commander. We had hot sweet tea served to us, and the commander thanked us for caring and told of some of their problems. The area was so vast that it was impossible to guard the whole perimeter, and occasionally raiding parties would get through and steal cattle and kill people, but fortunately taking few if any captives.

Commander Akot Deng Deng Akot said with a certain amount of pride, "The Arab traders can come here now without fear, because we (SPLA) are now in control, and they know we do not want to destroy humanity, but protect it." He told us that a thriving market was located nearby.

He then complained, "The Khartoum government gets help from other Arab nations with guns and ammunition and fuel. There is no one to help us. We have to capture our weapons and ammunition." He added somewhat belligerently, "We are not Muslims and will not become Muslims. Unless we fight to the last,

we will all be killed, and the Dinka people will be annihilated.
That's why you see me with a gun and in uniform. We have to
defend ourselves or we will die!"

He went on to say that they also wanted to bring peace to their
neighboring Arabs who have been manipulated by the NIF. Why
should so many people die?

He told of some of his exploits, which if they were even half
accurate, were remarkable with such little weaponry and so few
men—at least *we* saw only a few soldiers. I learned later that there
were hundreds of SPLA in the area waiting for their next offensive.

Caroline and John wanted to visit a site called Majak Bai where
two churches and a school were burned to the ground during a
raid just a few months before. Slaves had been taken as well.
Houses had also been pillaged and burned to the ground. It was
several miles beyond where we were to meet the slave traders.
Feeling tired, I really didn't want to add more miles to this trip.
But I felt it my duty.

When we got there, school was being taught under a big tree.
The only evidence of the church was the rain-washed ridges of
mud where the walls had been and the earthen "pews" in two
long, lumpy mud rows inside. The altar, or platform, was still
visible, and the ashes had not yet been totally washed away by the
recent rains. One Protestant and one Catholic church destroyed, as
well as the local school. I talked with the schoolteacher.

He told me he had about three hundred students before the
raid. Many had been taken as slaves. I asked about books and
teaching materials. He said they had all been burned in the school.
Nothing was left. That naturally left the question: "What are you
using to teach with?" His answer: "We can only teach what is in

our heads," he said while pointing at his own head. We have no books or blackboards, and we write in the sand..." I asked him how much he was being paid as a teacher. He said, "The GOS/NIF has closed all our schools down because we are Christians. I teach as a volunteer now...we all do!" I couldn't help but think of the teacher's strike for pay equity that was going on back in Ontario. These teachers had pay equity, they all received the same thing—nothing.

He looked across at his large class under the tree and pointed to them saying, "They are our future. We *must* teach them."

I left Majak Bai with a heavy heart. We went to our next stop, Aguat, where we were to meet the slave traders. When I got to Aguat, I had no idea where I was in relation to the town of Manyiel where we had stayed back in March. But the landscape was very similar. This time, the slave traders were there waiting for us under a big tree. There were two slave traders with 249 women and children sitting quietly except for some whispering and the whimpering of some babies.

While talking with the officials who had come with us, especially Angelo, I learned that these people had been living out in the open some miles away, waiting. They were being held until someone could pay their redemption price. They had just walked for three days without any food and very little water. One little boy had an open wound on his chest about three inches around. We learned it was from a beating he had received from his "owner" just before he had been bought back by the slave trader who brought him to us. The child, five or six years old, sat there quietly, uncomplaining, accepting whatever life brought to him. Again, I thought of my five-year-old grandson, Josh, and got a lump in my throat.

There were others who had scars. Faces were closed. With very few exceptions, their eyes were lifeless, hopeless, almost glazed with despair. A few of the boys' eyes still had some sparkle. I suspected they had been in slavery for a shorter time and had not yet experienced the total crushing of their spirits. They all sat staring at us. Six strangers—white people—sitting with the slave traders. What might have been going through their minds?

One of the traders explained, "I am not safe at my home anymore. They suspect what I am doing and burned down my house while I was away. I moved my family far away, and they are safe for now." They went on to tell about Hassan el Turabi bringing in groups from other Muslim countries to train the Popular Defense Force (PDF) which is made up of moderate Muslims who have been manipulated into joining with the NIF in raids against the black Christians and others of the south. They are told that it is not a crime to kill a non-Muslim.

Once again, we went through the counting of slaves, the counting of money, and the affirming to one another that we would do this again. Again it took over an hour and a half.

When the transaction was complete, and the traders moved off with their pockets full, we again talked to the group which we had just "bought." As before, Caroline together with John, told them what had been done. There was enthusiastic hand-clapping when they realized they were free. Caroline made the statement, "We will not stop doing this until every slave in Sudan is free."

Then Caroline introduced me as the man from Canada who had gathered the money from Canadian people to pay their redemption price.

When I stood in front of them, I had what some might call an epiphany. It was like a sudden revelation of what was really happening under this tree—clearly related to what had happened on a tree two thousand years ago. It all centered around the word "redemption."

I told them of the love of the Canadian people, and the sacrifice of their money to buy their freedom. They listened in silence. I then asked them if they knew the name of "Jesus." They looked at me in utter silence. Perhaps it was because of them recently being forced to accept Islam—they just sat there and stared at me.

I then went on to tell them that they were free; that they had been redeemed and were able to go back home with their families where they belonged. I then told them what redemption meant, using the example of Jesus who paid the sacrifice of His own life to redeem us back to God, where we belonged. I told them that was how much God loved them; that He gave His only Son to redeem them back to himself. I wanted them to understand as much as they could even though many of them were quite young. I wanted them to know that Jesus died for them, to save them. Then I again emphasized that they were free.

After that, the three journalists as well as Caroline and John began interviewing the newly redeemed slaves. Even though I am a total novice in the handling of a TV quality camera, I recorded as much footage for TV as I could. I also paused to listen in on some of the interviews.

Anton Christen, the Swiss journalist, roundly criticized me for "preaching" to the slaves. "You are doing exactly what the Muslims are doing, trying to convert them!" He seemed quite angry about it. I tried to explain that I *am* a preacher, and it is my responsibility before God to share the love of God. He would have none of it.

Finally, Lady Cox pointed out that, after all, it was "after" the fact that they were set free that I talked about Jesus. I had not tried to "force" anyone to become a Christian. Anton remained disturbed. I told him I was sorry he couldn't understand the difference between forcing and sharing my faith. Most of these people were from Christian families in any case.

The subject came up several times subsequently, and we finally agreed to disagree.

chapter thirteen

HEARTBREAKING STORIES

Caroline, John, and the journalists talked with some of the freed slaves. Following are some of the interviews, some of which I overheard in part, but which were documented, by Caroline Cox, John Eibner, or Linda Slobodian:

Ayen Deng Ding: Ayen was abducted from the village of Akek Rot near Marial Bai. Raiders came in 1993 and took Ayen and her ten-year-old daughter, Ajok Garang. Ayen was beaten (she showed her scars) and both were taken north to Abu Matarik. She was raped repeatedly during the march north. She was separated from her daughter Ajok and handed over to another man. Her daughter was held in a place not very far away.

While a slave she was raped by her owner. She witnessed the death of four other slaves by beatings: three young men and a woman. Others also were beaten severely but survived. She had lost hope of ever seeing her home again and just prayed. She was thrilled to be bought back and pleaded for her daughter to be brought back too. Ajok was also bought by the trader to bring back south with her mother. But many slaves were left behind.

Her husband had been killed in the raid, and she lives with relatives now, still harboring fear that she might be taken again.

She expressed deep gratitude for what CSI has done for her, but also expressed her concern for the many who are still slaves.

Abuk Atak: Three years ago her village of Palang, near Marial Bai, was raided and an Arab beat Abuk with a gun. Her eighteen-month-old daughter was lost in the raid and she has not seen her since. She was sold in the north in Abu Matarik in Southern Darfur to a man named Anur Mohammed. She was repeatedly raped, often more than once a day by different men. She often tried to resist but was beaten into submission. While she told her story, she fidgeted with some dry leaves in her hand and finally said, "I can't deny the facts. We were subjected to torture and suffering...I was circumcised...and...I can't deny our humiliation."

After another pause she said, "We were left with nothing after the raids; we lost our homes, our crops were burned, our cattle were stolen, and we don't even have any clothes." Another pause, and then, "...but there is no problem which we cannot endure."

Nyibol Yel Akuei: Nyibol had four children. Three starved to death. Her youngest is Abuk, her one surviving daughter who is a year old. They were abducted by the PDF (People's Defense Force) into slavery on May 16, 1997, from Majak Bai. Nyibol tells in her own words what happened:

> I was sitting in my compound early in the morning when armed men on horseback suddenly surrounded my home. There was no warning. I did not try to run away because there was no escape. One of the raiders lashed me and took me away with my baby. As we left I could see the raiders taking everything I owned and setting my house on fire. I was taken to another village for a few hours, then was forced to

carry a load of sorghum on my head. When I got tired and could not walk anymore, my captor, Mahmoud Abakor, took my child and tied her on a horse.

I walked for seven days to Abu Matarik. They made me work from morning 'til evening. My jobs were to carry water from the pump, clean the compound, and wash clothes. Mahmoud Abakor often insulted me, called me "slave," and he would beat me with a stick. He accused me of being lazy and refusing to obey orders. He...also used me as a concubine.

Mahmoud Abakor told me that I should practice Muslim prayers. I had trouble saying prayers in Arabic, so they gave me some training. Abuk, my child was renamed Miriam. I was never allowed to go from the compound.

Mahmoud Abakor had no other slaves at the compound, but he may have had some at his cattle camp, but I never saw them.

One day I was told to leave the compound with a trader. I was afraid to go. They told me I would go back to southern Sudan. I didn't believe them, but I had to go anyway.

I was happy to see you [white people] and to hear you speak so nicely to us, and that you are not going to do something terrible to us. My husband is now gone looking for food. When he comes back, we will find a new place to live....

Atoe Diing: Atoe is about 12 years of age. In May 1997 she was captured from the village of Majak Bai. She told part of her story:

We heard guns early in the morning. My mother told me to run quickly. We ran toward the river, but when we got there, we were surrounded by Arabs. We couldn't run anymore. My mother stopped and started to cry. One of the raiders came toward us and beat my mother. She fell down. I was taken away and put on a horse.

I was taken to different places before we reached Abu Matarik. It was there that my captor, Ali Abdullah, sold me to another man. After four days, I was sold again to another man who was called Mohammed. He took me to his home in a small village called Gumbildai, not far from Abu Matarik. I had to gather firewood, cook, and clean.

They gave me milk to drink every day, but some days they gave me no food at all. Mohammed's young sons were very rough with me and beat me. They tried to have sex with me but did not succeed.

Mohammed has many slaves. Most of them are in his cattle camp. He has three female slaves in his house.

Now that I am back, I will live with my sister. My mother went north to look for me and she has not come back. My father is dead.

The stories told by these newly freed slaves were similar, and in some cases almost identical to those we had released from slavery in March 1997. Scraps from the master's table were their food. Beatings. Rape. Mutilation by forced circumcision. Names changed to Arab names. They were forced to go to the mosque and pray in the Muslim manner and treated like animals.

We still had another destination in southern Sudan; there were yet more slaves to be redeemed. To get there we had to get back to the dirt airstrip which was at least sixteen kilometers away, near Nyamlel. It was too late to get back that evening so we got on our bikes and headed toward the church where we had slept during our first trip in March. I had the new bike and arrived first.

Since we were approaching the church from a completely different direction, and I had not seen the Lol River since we had crossed it early that morning when we left Nyamlel, I was actually in the church compound before I recognized it.

The others arrived in a straggling, tired line.

We set up our tents, choosing slight rises in the ground in case of rain. I couldn't help but laugh at Linda Slobodian. She had enough bug spray for the whole lot of us, plus a few more. She wasn't taking any chances. She was also catching on to how to get her tent up. This time I helped her, but she knew basically what loops and support rods went where.

We then gathered outside the church entrance to finally rest, eat some rations, and pump more clean water through the filters. The water from the Lol River was murky and clogged the pumps often. We had to take the filters out and scrape them, then continue pumping. Squirt by difficult squirt, the pumps produced crystal clear, clean water. We were already tired, but now our arms were sore. We finally pumped and filtered the water we would need for the next day's long trip.

I had hoped for an early start. But I had not figured on the determination of Caroline and John to try to promote peace between the local moderate Muslims and the Dinka tribe. They had arranged a meeting with the local Arab traders under a tree about a kilometer from the marketplace. Now I was beginning to understand the various approaches CSI was taking in trying to negotiate peace at the local level. They were committed to saving lives, bringing in desperately needed medicines, and redeeming slaves as an act of Christian compassion. They were also deeply committed to bringing out documented facts to set before a mysteriously silent world community regarding human rights in Sudan.

This meeting was much like the meeting the previous March. I sat and watched the faces of the Arab traders. They betrayed very little by their expression, but when they spoke it was clear they wanted peace. More recent documents and messages from Muslim leaders were read and passed out to the traders.

I was anxious to go. I seemed to be suffering perpetual exhaustion. I excused myself and borrowed a bike and went to the maketplace with a guide to wait for the others who "wouldn't be long."

It was a busy market, and although the Arab traders were not there, there were quite a few Dinka traders doing a brisk business. The heat was getting to me, and I asked for a place to rest. They took me into a market stall with a palm leaf roof and offered me a bed. I lay there and watched the marketplace. Here I was, a lone white man in the middle of what many might call "nowhere." But this was home to many people—people who have been living under persecution for a long time.

As I lay there waiting for the others, I thought of the fact that all the children below the age of fifteen had been raised all their lives under the threat of death. It was their normal expectation to live with fear and uncertainty. The relative peace that had come to this particular area was new. And it was a direct result of men and young boys who had decided enough was enough and took up arms. It was remarkable the array of arms and ammunition I had seen. I had been told several times that most of what they had is what they had captured when they carried out successful raids against the NIF army garrisons or police stations. They had captured a great many weapons when the NIF/GOS soldiers made raids—and lost.

But life had to go on. And trade was going on all around me in the market.

I was in a stall where tea was being sold. A little plastic scoop was filled, leveled off at the top, and tied into a little plastic packet. Sugar, beaded necklaces, batteries, and crudely sewn clothes were for sale, hanging in bright array near the front of the stall. A foot-pedaled Singer sewing machine was humming away behind me, making dresses and shirts from bright materials.

People stopped to stare at me, unblinking, but they usually flashed a quick smile before they moved on. John, Caroline, Linda, Pierre, and Anton were delayed back at the "meeting tree." I must admit, I was getting rather impatient since the afternoon was advancing. I was afraid we'd not get away on time to arrive at Nyamlel before dark.

As I waited, a small herd of cattle was driven right through the middle of the market area. Occasionally a fully armed SPLA soldier walked through, totally ignored by everyone. Others who seemed like civilians wore handguns strapped to their waists. Some had rifles. An occasional spear was carried by others.

Yet an almost serene atmosphere pervaded the whole market. I
didn't find it too unlike the many marketplaces I had been in
when I lived in Kenya, although there were definitely fewer items
available.

No one was in a hurry—except me. I began to fidget, wondering if the others had begun the trip to Nyamlel, perhaps thinking I
had already gone. Several young men had engaged me in conversation. They wondered who I was. As soon as I acknowledged I
was with Lady Cox, they accepted me like a brother. I finally asked
one of them where the other white people were.

They led me back to another tree where final preparations
were being made to get under way to Nyamlel. Simon, the nurse
and medical officer, greeted me—"Uncle Cal is here!" I was getting
used to this new designation. I spotted my psychedelic-colored,
twenty-one speed bike and laid claim to it. "Saint" Paul padded a
bike rack for Linda to sit on while he pedaled her back to the river
crossing. Anton spurned the use of a bike and decided to walk
with John and Caroline. Pierre decided it was a good idea and
joined our pedaling team.

It was tough peddling, but a lot faster than walking. We rested
and drank water often. Occasionally there was confusion over
which path to take, and our guides had to ask the local people
directions. We went through wet bogs, and we floundered through
deep sand.

We were startled at one point to be joined by Anton on a bike
with another guide leading him. He looked at me, grinned and
said, "Your idea about bicycles was a good idea."

The sun was beginning to set. That happens quickly in the
tropics. "Saint" Paul said it wasn't far now, and I thought I recog-

nized the cliff on the far side of the Lol River in the distance. I was looking forward to my next stay in the "Nyamlel Hilton." It was slightly off to our right. I knew we should be going along the banks of the Lol River, also on our right, but as it got darker the cliff seemed too far to the right. I was beginning to feel uneasy.

We rounded a bend in the path, and there was no more path. We had reached the river. It didn't feel familiar at all. I looked across the river, and could barely see a small beach-like landing place on the other side.

Our guides had gotten lost, and we were at least two miles down river from where the canoe should be waiting. Here we were with six bicycles and six people and a wide, fast-flowing river between us and the opposite shore. We had to get across if we were to sleep in our tents that night. Darkness was settling fast. We all sat down on the bank on tree roots feeling a bit discouraged. Being tired, and now lost, with no way of crossing the river was not conducive to peace of mind. Someone said, "Now what will we do?" as though one of us might have an answer. I quietly prayed, "Lord, help us!"

I had hardly lifted my head when a man suddenly and quietly appeared from the rushes to our right in a North American style canoe. It had the UN logo on one end. I whispered, "Thank you, Lord." We all breathed a sigh of relief. But still, a fourteen foot canoe, six people, six bicycles, and our day packs...and a wide swiftly flowing river...and a quickly setting sun.

The bikes were shuttled across first with the paddler fighting the current to reach the small landing on the other side. It seemed to take forever. Then he returned for us, and we gingerly climbed in. I was sitting very uncomfortably in the wet mud in the bottom to make it as stable as possible. Linda sat in the front with her back to the shore we wanted to reach. I sat immediately in front of her, with Pierre, Anton, and the paddler behind. The canoe was dangerously low in the water. It wasn't built for five people. The fact that "Saint" Paul had gone across with the bikes made it only a little better.

Linda sat as rigidly as though she was nailed into place. This was the gal who had never camped in her life before. She knew nothing about balance in a canoe. I just told her not to try to correct the balance—the paddler would do that. We launched; and again, it seemed to take forever. Darkness had descended, but the moon was casting some light on the water. As we approached the opposite shore I saw something break the surface of the water. Too slow for a fish. Crocodile...I knew of course that there would be both crocodile and hippo in the river.

I didn't mention it to Linda until we were safely on shore, but when I did, she almost fainted. She sat on a rock with her head in her hands but not before she asked if there were spiders there!

Our bicycles were gone. Just as well, there was no way we could have used them in the dark, and the path was steep. As we got to the top of the bank, St. Paul told us that a "Commander Paul" wanted us to stop at his SPLA quarters for coffee before we went on to Nyamlel. I had a few questions which went through my mind, "How many commanders in the SPLA were named Paul?" and even more important, "How far had we to walk before we reached Nyamlel?"

We stopped only for a moment, excusing ourselves from having coffee although we sat and chatted for a while. Anton began to question the commander about the number of troops he had, what weaponry he had and what plans they had for future military movement. He asked who was supplying them with arms and ammunition. I could understand his journalistic instincts in asking these questions, and he did so rather insistently. The commander just smiled in the lamplight and evaded the questions. What commander would tell a correspondent what most certainly were considered military secrets?

This Commander Paul gave us three armed SPLA soldiers to escort us back to Nyamlel, and walked with us a short distance into the darkness of the bush. I took the opportunity to apologize for the questions he had been asked about the SPLA resources and plans. He just smiled and patted me on the shoulder. About a half kilometer from his headquarters, he left us in the care of his soldiers, told us we would be safe, and turned back to his camp.

I knew from my first trip approximately where we were. We should pass the demolished Catholic mission on our right, then come to Nyamlel about two miles beyond that. We never did see the church compound. For that matter, we saw only two lights in the distance.

The path was rough, and the soldiers walked at a fast clip. Too fast for all of us out-of-condition whites. They slowed down for us. We stumbled over murram rocks; trees and bushes brushed at us as we passed. I stayed behind Linda to make sure she wasn't left behind. She was totally exhausted. She asked that we slow down even more. The path wound in several directions around gullies and over little hills and through thick bush. It was only the occasional sight of the moon that assured me we were still going in the same direction.

I also trusted the soldiers who knew the area well…until they

pointed ahead…and left us on our own. I looked ahead. I knew
there should be a light at Nyamlel, but saw none. Since I was the
only one who had been in the area before, I knew at least that the
River Lol was, or should be, on our right. I reasoned, "If the path
divides, we keep right, and keep the moon in the same place in
the sky." The path did divide, several times.

At one point we passed a house with a light shining inside. No
movement. Not a sound. We stepped silently by and continued,
hopefully in the right direction. When we had almost given up
hope of finding Nyamlel, I gradually began to realize I felt in familiar territory. I wanted to turn left, but Anton and Pierre wanted to
keep on the right. It made sense in theory, but I was still convinced we were close to the "Nyamlel Hilton."

Linda followed me, and Anton and Pierre started down the
path that I knew now would lead them to the bottom of the cliff
below the "Nyamlel Hilton." Even though I could see nothing, I
yelled down to them, "This is the way, I'm sure of it." Anton and
Pierre cut across to our path and joined Linda and me in the darkness.

Suddenly I saw the dim outline of a roof against the sky. Then
a light appeared, dim, but right where it should be. As we came
up over the rise I recognized "home." When we walked into the
compound of the now familiar "Nyamlel Hilton," John Eibner,
Caroline Cox, and Angelo stood and said, with what sounded like
delight, "Uncle Cal!"

They had been preparing their food for the evening meal. They
said they had been worried about us and had sent out several
search parties.

We four just sat down with great sighs of relief.

Pitching a tent in the dark is not a lot of fun, especially when you are exhausted from heat and more exercise than anyone cares to have. We finally settled down for the night, had some army rations, and went to sleep knowing, or at least hoping that the plane would actually arrive the next day.

chapter fourteen

THE LAST TRADE

The Cessna Caravan arrived the next morning on schedule. We packed our gear and had some food from our rations, and then met several people who had walked a long distance to see Caroline and John who had been instrumental in paying for their redemption in previous trips.

There was also a young women of twenty-three, who, with her twins, had just returned from Kenya where she and one of her babies had received urgent medical attention after being evacuated by CSI to Lokichokio by air in June after a raid on her home in May of 1997. The Red Cross had not been able to evacuate her because Khartoum had designated that whole area of Bahr el Ghazal as a "no go" area. Many, many innocent civilians died simply because they could not get medical help. Many died slowly and painfully.

Adel Lake was from Majak Bai. Even as I listened to her story, it was hard to imagine the horror of what she went through. She told us: "When the army came, we were in our tukul (house) when we heard gunshots. I grabbed my twins who were one month old, and ran. I couldn't carry my three-year-old son, Wek Wol, so he ran behind me. We tried to hide in the bush, but the

Arabs saw us and shot at us. I saw my son fall. I was shot in the leg and fell. The bone was fractured." She went on to tell how the Arabs had tried to take her twins, but she fought with them, and they stabbed her. She lost consciousness.

Later, when she regained consciousness, she was told by others who had survived the raid that her son, Wek Wol, was in her *tukul* when it was set on fire. He was burned to death. She was surprised to find she still had her twins, but a bullet which had hit her, had also hit the foot of one of them. Her sister-in-law had been shot dead.

She expressed gratitude to CSI and those who made it possible for her to get to Kenya for medical help. She would have died in the hut where she was found by chance by CSI personnel during a heavy rainfall. They had gone into the hut they thought was empty and found Adel near death. Operations on her thigh and on her twin's foot saved them both. Adel can walk and has some pain still, but her baby's foot will never be normal.

She said that she had been told her husband was alive and was trying to find food and would be coming to Nyamlel for her soon.

We walked the few kilometers to the airstrip as soon as we heard the Cessna fly overhead. We voiced some fond farewells, and Angelo said, "Uncle Cal, we will see you again." Not a question, a statement. We boarded the plane, and took a short flight to another dirt airstrip at Malwal Akon. We were met there by a large group of people and two vehicles, one with neither cab nor windshield. One vehicle carried our baggage and we tumbled into the back of the other. This was the camp of Commander Paul Malong Awan of the SPLA. It seemed the population here was larger, but there also seemed to be a much more relaxed atmosphere.

The trucks dropped us off at the entrance to a large, very well kept compound. We all grabbed our gear and were ushered inside where we sat around a table in the open under a massive tree. Tea was served with chicken and "other things." I noticed Linda only pretending to eat a little. She leaned down and fed a bone to a scrawny pup.

The rest of us ate with some enthusiasm. There was even fresh-baked bread. Part of our enthusiasm may have been based on the fact that there were vehicles here, and we wouldn't have to walk many miles. We heard several trucks and pickups driving near and around the compound. It had a "safe" feel.

The time came to meet the slave trader and redeem some more slaves. I grabbed my TV camera. I had given my 35mm camera to Linda several days earlier because the one she had stopped working. She loaded new film, and with John, Caroline, Pierre, and Anton, we headed for the gate of the compound expecting to clamber into the back of a pickup. We were told we would walk. Oh no...!

It turned out to be less than a few hundred meters. We ducked under the low hanging branches of a big tree and saw about two hundred boys between the ages of five and perhaps twelve. No girls. No women, except standing in the background away from the boys. We all wondered what was going on. Could this be a setup? Would we be paying money for a bunch of boys that were already paid for or perhaps never actually taken as slaves?

Slowly, the whole story emerged. Most of these boys had already been redeemed by their families and villages, and some of them had been home for some time. Apparently this area was more prosperous.

We met the slave trader who looked like an African, yet...not quite. He used the name "Ahmed" which we took to be an alias. He told us his story. He looked to be about thirty years old and seemed very much at home with everyone around him. Almost too much at home...until we heard his story.

His father was an Arab and his mother a Dinka. When his father died a year or so earlier, he had left "Ahmed" a large inheritance. There had been slave raids in the Malwal Akon area, and many Dinka women and children had been taken captive. Among them were two sons of his mother's sister. She came to him and begged him to find her two sons, "Ahmed's" cousins, and buy them back. He agreed to try. He tracked them down, bought them back, and returned them to his aunt, their mother.

The people in this area had more cattle and "wealth" (although that is a comparative word, totally unrelated to wealth as we know it in North America). Other parents came to him and commissioned him to get back their children. It was a dangerous undertaking, but he took on the job and began to retrieve children. He told us that he would only go to cattle camps where the boys were most often used. He used as his excuse that he was buying them to work with his own cattle. He considered it too dangerous to his own life to try to retrieve women and girls, since they were usually in Arab's homes and used as domestic slaves and as concubines.

As a result he had been able to redeem about 150 boys for those who could afford to pay the cost. We found that there were forty-five in this group of about two hundred who had not been paid for because the families were too poverty-stricken to pay the cost. They had been allowed to return to their families, but the debt was outstanding, and "Ahmed" had his inheritance tied up in these boys.

John Eibner and I took the forty-five boys to an open area in another place away from the tree. We went through a list, name by name, having them stand when their name was called. I counted them several times and there were more than forty-five. Yet the list had only forty-five names. Several who had joined the group but whose names were not on the list of unredeemed boys, were sent back to the group under the tree. They had apparently misunderstood the instructions regarding who should come with us.

Meanwhile, Pierre, Linda, and Anton remained with those under the tree to get their stories. Caroline Cox also stayed to question those who had already been redeemed by their own families.

I was not about to pay for someone who was already free. When we had an accurate count, and established that the forty-five, by name, were the right ones, we went back into the commander's compound. Caroline and the three journalists joined John and I, and with Commander Malong and "Ahmed," John and I paid for the forty-five boys. They were now all free.

One particular story related to me later by Linda Slobodian, and written up in the CSI report of this trip was the most horrifying I had yet heard.

The story was told by a young boy called Geng Kwak Atiang. When the raid had taken place three years previously, he was with two other boys when they were captured. One of the boys put up such a fuss, refusing to go, that the raiders put him in a mortar and beat him to death with a pestle. Geng was then taken toward the north in a group of fifteen boys. Three tried to escape and were thrown into a well and drowned.

Later, two others, either for some disobedience or for trying to escape, had both their hands and their feet cut off. The other boys tried to feed them and nurse them, but they died. Geng was visibly upset as he recounted this experience. As Geng told this story, Linda described how he seemed to relive it all as he talked, and his hands fumbled with a dead leaf.

Geng was taken north and sold to a man called Kamis Ibrahim from Darfur. He was kept at a camp where he had to care for goats and cattle. His name was changed to Ahmed, but he was never taken to the mosque because he had to work all the time.

When the trader came to retrieve him to bring him south, he was terrified he would be caught or that it was a trick, and that he would have his hands and feet cut off. While he was in captivity, his father was killed by the PDF. Only his mother survived.

"Ahmed," the slave retriever, told us there were another seventeen who had not been paid for. I told John I would not pay for slaves I did not see. During this whole process, several hours had passed and another meal was brought to us. We talked with "Ahmed" and the commander until dusk. Before he left, "Ahmed" announced that he would not ask any further payment for the seventeen. He would free them himself. We parted company after dark, then headed for our tents, and went to bed.

When I woke up the next morning, it was to a loud shout— "Shut up!" I burst out in laughter. I heard the shout again; it was in English with a French Canadian accent. Pierre was shouting at the top of his voice. I looked out the flap of my tent, and there was Pierre shouting up into the massive tree overhead at some tropical birds which were, admittedly, making some pretty loud and annoying cries. What's more, I was feeling rested. I had done a minimum of walking during the last twenty-four hours. We had accomplished our mission—or, at least, I had accomplished *my* mission—294 slaves set free. Wow!

WARAWAR MARKET

W e still had one more trip to make. The plane was scheduled to return to pick us up midafternoon. Meanwhile, the commander wanted to take us, by truck, to a large marketplace in which he held a certain justifiable pride. It was called Warawar. We jumped into the back of the two pickups with the SPLA flags on their windshields and headed out. We had a good number of SPLA soldiers, fully armed, with us.

It was an interesting drive. Everything and everyone seemed joyful. People came running from thatched houses as we went by and waved as the two pickups passed. We hung on for dear life. There was no road, just flat land with a few boggy areas which we skirted. Vehicles had passed here before, but it certainly had no right to be called a road. We passed groups of armed and uni-formed SPLA soldiers going back toward Malwal Akon. We saw no wildlife, but there was evidence of some.

When we pulled into Warawar market, I was stunned at the size of it. And I saw Africans and Arabs working side by side in market stalls. We parked under the largest tree in sight and were led on a walking tour through the streets of this thriving place. Commander Malong unabashedly took credit for bringing peace to the area, and he was greeted happily by both Africans and Arabs alike.

It was a fascinating place. The streets were lined with bazaar-type, open stalls displaying an amazing array of goods for sale. Freshly slaughtered beef and goat meat hung from stout branches in the "butcher shops." The hoards of flies settling on the meat didn't seem to bother anyone but we squeamish whites. Some things smelled good, some things just plain smelled. The head of a cow was sitting on a makeshift table—for sale.

In the middle of one wide street were two very large ovens made of clay. Fire glowed hotly inside, and the smell of fresh bread filled the air. The whole place was busy. We were shown the cattle pens where cattle were brought to market one day each week. Commander Malong seemed proud of the peaceful but high energy of the whole marketplace. I recognized sugar cane growing in several yards, papaya trees, and there were quite a few chickens pecking about in the streets and under the tables in the market stalls. It made me feel almost at home.

Plastic shoes were beside peanuts, little red peppers, coffee in open piles, and even stick matches. It was amazing what was available. Salt, cooked food in little open, not-very-clean...I hesitate to call them...restaurants.

Our tour came to an end, and we were all led to a large clearing overshadowed by four or five mango trees. Chairs had been set out. We were asked to be seated and given the hot sweet tea once again. Arabs began to trickle in, some carrying chairs. SPLA soldiers stood both within the circle that was formed, and outside the area, with rifles at the ready. It looked like another peace talk was about to take place.

The Arabs were members of the Rizeiqat and Misiriyah tribes. After Caroline said a few words, Commander Malong spoke. He told of the willingness of the Arabs to voluntarily come here to trade. He complimented them that, when some of their Arab brothers had done a cattle raid, the other peace-loving Arabs had retrieved the cattle, returning them to their rightful owners. Malong said, "This shows they know right from wrong."

Then Commander Malong invited the Arabs to speak their minds. We heard it all through interpreters, members of the black Dinka tribe. I was quite impressed with the attitude the Arabs showed. They were happy at the peace which had come to the Warawar area. They expressed gratitude to CSI for bringing Mubarak el Mahdi to visit them some time in the recent past.

This was all a part of the political peacemaking process, and the Arabs spoke of their gratitude that they could live and trade here without fear. They made it abundantly clear that they felt that the Riziqat and Misiriyah tribes were good neighbors with the Dinka, and that they had many marriage ties. They also said that, though problems did arise from time to time, they could work them out together without the interference of Khartoum.

They made the point again, "When we are at war, we all die, both Arabs and Dinkas." They informed us that, although the NIF was able to convince a few of their people to join in their fight against the Dinkas, they were not getting enough now to cause such problems as before.

Our trip back to Malwal Akon was no more comfortable than the drive to the marketplace. It was about twenty kilometers each way. When we got back to Malwal Akon, we were driven straight to the airstrip where our gear, and the Cessna were both waiting for us. After final farewells, we boarded and flew back to Lokichokio in Kenya. Cold pop was on board, along with refreshing sandwiches and fruit.

We stayed overnight again in the TrackMark camp where a good hot meal and a shower put me out like a light. The following day we flew back to Nairobi where Pierre, Linda, and I checked in to a clean hotel. Pierre and Linda had made their own arrangements for their return to Canada.

I had several meetings with officials of the SRRA/SPLM regarding the feeding program I was involved in through Ethiopia. Caroline Cox and John Eibner joined me in the meeting with Dr. Justin Yaac of the SPLM and Dr. Haruun L. Ruun, the executive secretary of the New Sudan Council of Churches. Al Kehler of the Canada Food Grains Banks was there as well as Bob Haarzager of the Mennonite Central Committee.

We discussed the use of the funds raised through *100 Huntley Street* and came to agreement as to how we would work through the existing infrastructures in both Kenya and Ethiopia to get the food into the Blue Nile province of Sudan.

I had a hamburger and chips with Pierre and Linda that evening after dark near the hotel's pool.

We rehearsed our several days together in Sudan and discussed several points of interest to all of us which we were not quite sure how to interpret. We finally separated and headed for our own rooms. Before I went to bed, I was delighted to have a visit from my good friend Don Matheny with three of his daughters. He told me what God was doing in the various churches in Nairobi.

The church my father had built back in 1960 was now a con-

gregation of ten thousand with branch churches and African missionaries being sent throughout Kenya. Don was heading a church
so large they were meeting in the stadium and had started hundreds of "cell groups" throughout the city.

When I arrived home in Canada, I was heat-exhausted and jet-
lagged. But the next day I was right back into the stride of things
at the office. Mail had piled up, appointments had been made, and
there were other urgent matters to attend to, including redesigning
the curriculum of the School of Broadcasting. My staff carried the
brunt of that load. I also had to write and prerecord a large number of my daily commentaries. Life began to feel a bit like a pressure cooker. And I wasn't quite prepared for what came next.

chapter sixteen

DEATH THREATS

I had been dealing with the threat of death for months now. Sudanese threatened by death during slave raids in the Bahr el Ghazal area of southern Sudan. Hundreds of thousands of people facing the threat of death by starvation in the Blue Nile region. But now it came home.

On Friday, October 24, 1997, Pierre Richard published the first in a three-day series of eight pages, ending in the Sunday edition of *Le Journal De Montreal*. This newspaper has the largest French readership in Canada.

On Monday, October 27, I received a telephone call from a very sober sounding Pierre Richard. I had grown to like Pierre a great deal during our trip together in the Sudan and was glad to hear from him. But he had some bad news to pass on. He had received two anonymous letters in the mail, one stating who his greatest enemy was, and he gave the Arabic name of someone living in Montreal. The other was a threat. He gave these letters to his editor.

Within another day or two, he received a very clear threat against his own life. Lady Cox, John Eibner, and I were also threatened. The letter was not mailed to him, but came to his attention through a person who sneaked a photocopy of it to Pierre saying in a handwritten note, "I do not agree with the system of slavery and the Arabic religion which is why…when somebody asked me to copy five pages, I did more especially for you."

I have a photocopy of the letter calling for our elimination. It is unsigned, but the name of the author is typed at the bottom. It was in French. Pierre turned this over to his editor, and the Royal Canadian Mounted Police were called.

The RCMP recognized the name at the bottom of the letter. They went to this person who denied any knowledge of the letter. They are watching him very closely because he is known as a radical fundamentalist Muslim who apparently has some strong connections with Sudan. The letter was addressed to Dr. Hassan el Turabi (leader of the National Islamic Front in Sudan).

I quote below, several paragraphs as they were translated from French:

> *We must find together, the sure power to be certain that the journalist and the collaborators from CCCI [Crossroads Christian Communications Inc.] and International Christian Solidarity who participated in this report are eliminated so that they cannot continue in the future to harm Sudan authority and our fight in the South against the enemy of Islam.*

The next two paragraphs were translated for me as follows:

> *It is very important that we take quick exemplary measures to quiet Pierre Hughes Richard as he is a friend of the south,*

so that the campaign of the breakdown against the Sudan will be finished as quickly as possible.

As well as Pierre Hughes, the Baroness Caroline Cox, and John Eibner from the International Christian Solidarity and Calvin Bombay of Crossroads and the Commander Paul Malong, responsible for a division of the APLS and the Commissioner Aleu Jok responsible for West Aweil who work together by their actions and statements against the Sudan.

Another paragraph said:

I am convinced that we must quickly define the problems caused by Crossroads and International Christian Solidarity and correct these errors immediately. This job can be executed by our common friends.

Obviously, Pierre's articles stirred up a hornet's nest.

I sent copies of everything to both John Eibner and Lady Cox, both of whom contacted their appropriate security authorities. These threats have been taken seriously in all three countries—Canada, Switzerland, and England.

I also sought the advice of Ontario Provincial Police, and they visited me in my home. They told me there was little they could do, "until something happened." Scant assurance that is! But I have been grateful for a few slow OPP cruisers going past my house from time to time.

Am I afraid? No! Definitely not afraid. Cautious? Yes. Some suggested it might be wise not to go back to Sudan again. They may feel they are right in this recommendation, but when I have seen and heard what I know to be the truth of what is happening in the south of Sudan, how can I, as a Christian just suddenly and coldly switch off compassion? That just doesn't work with me.

And then of course, there is that wonderful promise from God's Word in Psalm 41:1–2.

On November 2, an eight-day series on slavery in Sudan was published by the *Calgary Sun*. The articles were written by Linda Slobodian and took the main part of thirty-six pages. I marveled at this diminutive little journalist who was afraid of spiders, but was fearless in writing her account of the trip through Sudan. She too received a few nasty calls, and like the rest of us, is living on the edge.

EPILOGUE

In January 1998, I attended the MissionsFest in Vancouver, British Columbia. We had a booth depicting not only the slavery involvement of Crossroads, but our School of Broadcast, The W.H.E.A.T. fund, as well as our Emergency Response and Development Fund, in other areas of activity.

I was asked to speak for a few minutes in the main session on the Sunday morning, just before the keynote speaker. There was utter silence as I gave my report. At that point I was acutely aware of the threats that had been made against my life. I found myself consciously scanning the crowd for possible danger. Yet, I made reference to Psalm 41:1–2 and made the statement that, "I am confident that I am bulletproof until God is done with me, and He is not done with me yet!" This caused loud applause from the crowd.

I expected people to come to our booth at the MissionsFest display hall, so I quickly had some fast-food and went to the booth. Our booth was well manned. My son, John, had come to videotape interviews with people which we would later use on *100 Huntley Street* and for the documentary we would produce on Sudan. My daughter, Elaine, then studying linguistics in Trinity Western University had come to help. Two other staff members from *100 Huntley Street* had also come, David Butcher and Russ Johnson.

Linda Slobodian had also come from Calgary bringing some large photographs from Sudan which she had taken with the camera I had lent her.

Many people came by asking many questions of Linda and I. As I was answering some questions I noticed a group of three black people coming, notably a man who was probably six-foot-eight-inches tall.

He looked me in the eye and asked, "Are you Cal Bombay?" I said I was. He put his big arms around me and hugged me, weeping gently. He then held me by the shoulders in his big hands, backed off and looked me in the face again. He said, "Thank you." Slightly at a loss as to how to respond, I simply said, "I love your people." He answered, "You don't even have to say it," and he hugged me again.

His wife, also well over six feet tall, then stepped up to me and hugged me, repeating over and over again, "Thank you...thank you...thank you..." and weeping in a choked voice.

After a few emotional moments, I turned to the man and asked his name. He said he was Riel Chut from Bahr el Ghazal. He told me that he had been a lawyer in Sudan, but had to flee to Egypt in 1991 with his wife, Gema, who is a pharmacist. There was no law left to practice in Sudan, and precious little medicine in any case. He had worked with Campus Crusade in Egypt for a time, but had now come to Canada, and was looking for work.

He could not practice law in Canada without requalifying under Canadian Bar requirements. They had been in Vancouver for three months.

Meanwhile, the older woman, in a heavy winter coat was standing back looking at me. I turned my attention to her. As she moved toward me, her face crumbled into sobs. She put her arms around me sobbing uncontrollably. She clung to me for about ten minutes, her whole body racked with sobs. I wept as well, sensing her unspoken anguish.

Riel turned his back to the people around the booth, facing into a corner, pulled a handkerchief from his pocket and kept wiping his eyes as the old brokenhearted woman sobbed and clung to me.

Later, the old lady sat with Linda Slobodian and told her story. I heard some of it. She was a part of a family connection of about two hundred individuals in the typical African extended family. She was fortunate to be with Riel and Gema who are a part of the family connection. I'm not sure where she fit into the extended family, since that would include brothers, sisters, cousins, aunts and uncles on both sides of Riel and Gema's families.

I never heard her name. But she wept as she related how that, of the approximate two hundred family connections, Riel and Gema were the only ones she knew were safe. She didn't know where any of the others were. Perhaps some were still in Bahr el Ghazal. Some were most certainly dead. Some were probably taken as slaves. Others may have fled to who knows where? She sat for more than a half hour, pouring out her heart to Linda who held her hand tenderly. It was difficult, even though I had been in Bahr el Ghazal, to relate to the devastation of soul in this broken woman.

That whole experience with Riel, Gema, and that old mother, with their words and tears of thanks made all the risks I had taken worthwhile.

My activities in Sudan have opened doors I would never have dreamed possible.

In March 1998, I received an invitation to speak at the Canadian National Prayer Breakfast in the Confederation Building in Ottawa, Canada's Capital City. The prayer breakfast was being organized by the Hon. Paul Steckle, MP, together with his Executive Assistant, Terry Puerstl. Through the visit of Baroness Cox and myself to Ottawa regarding the situation in Sudan, Terry came into a renewed and close walk with the Lord Jesus Christ. Ambassadors from about seventy countries around the world attended. And about a third of the members of the House of Commons were there. Paul Henderson, who had become a Christian after his famous goal which won the series just 34 seconds before the end of the last game, gave a clear and pointed testimony of his having found Jesus Christ as his personal Savior. Prime Minister Jean Chretien sat six feet in front of the podium, listening intently, in spite of a controversial upcoming visit to Cuba to confront Castro with some human rights issues.

Following the breakfast, I was one of three speakers in a seminar on leadership. I mentioned that the success of any nation depends on its practice of justice and righteousness, and that Christians in Parliament have a non-partisan obligation to do what their common Christian convictions, biblically based, dictated they should do. I mentioned that it would be better to be a victim of the result of a decision based on truth and justice, than to be successful through illegitimate means. One day, they will face not just their constituency, but God Himself in the final judgment.

"Blessed is that nations who's God is the Lord." I put the case forward for obedience to God and His word being of prime importance. I mentioned Sudan as an example of a country gone mad when led by people who despised those who called themselves Christian. A god of hatred and violence, as opposed to God of love.

Throughout the whole period of the prayer breakfast, which included a dinner the night before the breakfast, Jesus Christ was presented without apology as the hope of both individuals and of the nation. Several who had attended for several years running said it was the most Christ-centered prayer breakfast they had ever attended. In years past, a syncretistic 'god' had been the center of the prayers. The Christians in Parliament were delighted with the overt presentation of Jesus as the only hope of mankind.

I met more Christian Members of Parliament of the various political parties than I had known existed. It produced in me a new hope, and renewed optimism about the future of Canada. For two weeks previously we had been addressing the matter of examining and rebuilding the Christian foundations of Canada on the *100 Huntley Street* television program.

At the end of the seminar on leadership, David Kilgour sought me out and thanked me for the timely challenge. He also told me that a man had been in contact with him the day before who had just returned from Sudan. He told David Kilgour that the regime in Khartoum would soon fall. David Kilgour gave me his name and telephone number and said that I should contact him as soon as possible. He added, "And tell him I told you to call him."

When I returned to Toronto, I telephoned Omar Mahmoud (not his real name). He was delighted to receive my call and said that he and David Kilgour had discussed my activities in the south of Sudan.

He told me he is a Muslim, and that he had been watching
100 Huntley Street and was well aware of what I had been doing in
Sudan. It was a long conversation. He had just successfully got his
wife and children out of Sudan with the help of some "friends." He
had been a professor in the University in Khartoum for fourteen
years but is now attached to the University of Toronto.

He then went on to tell me that he had been elected as executive secretary of the Sudan Alliance Forces. I asked him what that
was. He answered, "It is a coalition of the Muslim dissidents of the
north, all Muslim, who are forming a military force to oppose
the regime in Khartoum." He referred to the rogue regime in
Khartoum, not as "fundamentalist," but as "absolutist." In this connection he stated that their desire was that a democratic government of a secular nature would replace the present regime. He
believes in separation of religion and state.

The Sudan Alliance Forces will work in harmony with the
Sudan People's Liberation Army of the south to bring the
Khartoum absolutist regime to an end.

I asked him how long he thought the present regime would
last. He answered, "If it lasts two years, it will be a miracle. If it
lasts even a year, I will be surprised!" I told him that I had been
predicting that the Khartoum regime would fall before the end of
1998. The Khartoum regime's only hope would be in importing
major military force from supportive Muslim fundamentalist governments.

At the moment, the regime of Hassan el Bashir and Omar el
Turabi are conscripting school children whose average age is thirteen years. They have announced that they will conscript 250,000
in the first year, and 650,000 in the next three years.

An incident at an army training camp near the Nile across from Egypt was recently reported, where 260 children had been gunned down by the NIF forces when they tried to escape to Egypt. The regime in Khartoum claimed there were about fifty-five who had "drowned" as they tried to desert when their boat overturned. One lad who made good his escape told his story to the press, telling how they had been shot at mercilessly, and he swam past many bodies to get to the opposite shore of the Nile.

When I mentioned this incident, Omar said that the Nile is shallow there and there would not even be a boat that would hold twenty people, let alone fifty-five, much less 260. In Khartoum, the Muslim mothers of these conscripted youths put on demonstrations which were broken up by the military forces of Omar el Turabi.

Omar Mahmoud ended our telephone conversation with a request to meet with me when we both returned from Africa near the end of June 1998. (I went to visit four African nations to recruit students for our School of Broadcast.) Omar was going back to Sudan during the same time period to help organize the militia of the new Sudan Alliance Forces.

The Khartoum government is using these young "recruits" as war fodder. They are disallowed jobs or further education until they have served three years in the army. It sounds to me like a regime in desperate straits.

Even as you read this book, hundreds of thousands of southern Sudanese citizens are starving to death—all the direct result of a predatory and despotic religious fanaticism. Already it is estimated that more than 1.5 million have died. The United Nations is calling for immediate emergency aid to be forthcoming from any and every country in the world. There has been minimal response, although awareness is rising.

When the present wicked regime has been replaced by some form of democratic government, there will be an ongoing need for several years for emergency food aid, as well as long-term development aid. The inaction of the world to what is happening in Sudan should weigh heavily on the conscience of everyone who knows about the situation. The Scripture in 1 John 3:17 comes to mind: "But whoever has this world's goods and sees his brother in need, and shuts up his heart from him, how does the love of God abide in him?"

Meanwhile, the terror, starvation, and poverty increases in southern Sudan. Recent reports by the United Nations predict inevitable starvation of hundreds of thousands of people. Every relief agency trying to get food, seed, and farming instruments into southern Sudan is frustrated by the flight restrictions imposed by the repressive regime in Khartoum. They are using starvation as a weapon against the Bahr el Ghazal area particularly because of the fact that the Dinka people are predominantly Christian.

The black population in southern Sudan hear rumors of a flight coming in with food and walk for miles and days to get to the airstrip only to find that either there was no flight, or the food has all been distributed before they arrive. Desperate mothers hold listless babies dying in their arms.

Although some actions have been taken by the Canadian and United States governments, I am convinced that in both cases the actions fall woefully short in their attention to the situation in Sudan. More can and should be done.

When the regime in Khartoum falls, as it surely will, there will still be desperate needs in the south of Sudan. Seed and farming implements will be needed. Wells will need to be reopened, and many new wells drilled. Training in hygiene, agriculture, and formal education will be desperately needed. The population has been displaced for so long that a whole generation of young people know nothing but terror, homelessness, war, and starvation.

Schools and churches will have to be rebuilt. The *intelligencia* now living in exile who were fortunate enough to escape with their lives will have to be reintegrated into the south with their expertise.

There will still be slaves in the hands of Arab owners in the north who will need to be set free. It is hoped that a democratically elected government would address this immediately when in power. Law and order needs to be restored, not based on Sha'ria law with its violent interpretations, but on the basis of basic human rights for every citizen in Sudan.

Meanwhile, the fanatical, fundamentalist Muslim religious dictatorship needs to be challenged, both by governments and by the United Nations...and by you. Pressure can be applied. Up to this point, the regime in Khartoum has disregarded world opinion. I believe that this will be their undoing and that they will fall.

§

WHAT CAN BE DONE?

1) Pray for the beleaguered people of the various tribes of the southern Sudan. Ask the Lord what YOU should do about it. Imagine yourself in that situation. Make it personal by realizing how you would feel if it was your husband, wife, children who were being beaten, raped, treated like animals, and all too often, killed.

2) In kindly words, but in a firm way, let your representative in government know your opinion about the violation of human rights against the people of Sudan; violations that are perpetrated and encouraged by their own government.

3) Write to the United Nations and ask for the report by Dr. Gasper Biro, special Rappoteur for the United Nations, which was submitted to the Commission of Human Rights according to resolution 1996/73. This is a 21-page document.

4) When you receive and read the above document, contact your local news media and ask why so little is being said about such atrocities. Ask that they do their own research and disseminate their findings. Give them a copy of the United Nations report by Dr. Biro.

5) Financially support any mission or agency which is trying

to feed the starving and/or free slaves, or which is working to expose these evils to the eyes of the world community.

ADDRESSES TO WRITE ASKING FOR TRADE EMBARGOES AND MORE RESOLUTE ACTION ON HUMAN RIGHTS IN SUDAN

The Hon. Jean Chretien

Prime Minister

House of Commons

Ottawa, ON K1A 0G2

The Hon. Lloyd Axworthy

Minister of Foreign Affairs

House of Commons

Ottawa, ON K1A 0G2

(613) 995-1851

Mr. John Scholfield

Department Policy Advisor

to Minister of Foreign Affairs

The Sudan Desk

125 Sussex Drive

Ottawa, ON K1A 0G2

Mr. Dennis Steven

Political Policy Advisor to the

Minister

House of Commons

Ottawa, ON K1A 0A6

(613) 994-6994

The Hon. David Kilgour

Secretary of State for Africa

125 Susses Drive

Lester B Pearson Building

Tower A, 8th. Floor

Ottawa, Ontario, K1A 0G2

(613) 992-6550

also:

Mr. Abdel Ghani Al Naim

Minister, Council, and Charge d'

Affairs for Sudan

85 Range Road Suite # 507

Ottawa, ON K1N 8J6

(613) 235-4000 or

(613) 235-4999

President Bill Clinton

The White House

Washington, DC 20500

E-mail can be sent via the

following website:

http://www.whitehouse.gov

MISSIONS AGENCIES
WHICH YOU COULD SUPPORT

Christian Solidarity Worldwide
P.O. Box 99, New Malden
Surrey
KT3 3YF, United Kingdom

World Vision
121 E. Huntington Drive
Monrovia, CA 91016
1-888-511-6593

Voice of the Martyrs
P.O. Box 443
Bartlesville, OK 74005-0443
(918) 337-8015

Samaritan's Purse
P.O. Box 3000
Boone, NC 28607

Emergency Response and Development Fund
c/o Crossroads Christian Communications
1295 North Service Road
Burlington, Ontario
Canada   L7R 4M2

Printed in the United States
by Baker & Taylor Publisher Services